The World of
Leonardo

TIME-LIFE LIBRARY OF ART

The World of Leonardo

1452-1519

by Robert Wallace
and
the Editors of TIME-LIFE BOOKS

TIME-LIFE INTERNATIONAL (NEDERLAND) N.V.

About the Author:

Robert Wallace is widely known as a staff writer for Time Inc. He has published more than 100 nonfiction articles as well as a number of short stories and poems. His first writing on art was an article about the Renaissance for LIFE's series "The History of Western Culture." He is the author of *Rise of Russia* for TIME-LIFE BOOKS' Great Ages of Man series, as well as *The World of Rembrandt* for the TIME-LIFE Library of Art. *The World of Leonardo* is the fruit of more than a year's intensive study in the museums and libraries of Europe.

The Consulting Editor:

H. W. Janson is Professor of Fine Arts at New York University, where he is also Chairman of the Department of Fine Arts at Washington Square College. Among his numerous books and publications are his definitive *History of Art,* which ranges from prehistory to the present day, *The Sculpture of Donatello* and *The Story of Painting for Young People,* which he co-authored with his wife.

The Consultant for This Book:

Marilyn Aronberg Lavin rendered invaluable assistance in the preparation of this book, reading the entire text and supplying expert advice. A leading scholar of Renaissance art history, she is the author of a number of articles on 15th and 16th Century painting and iconography as well as a study on 17th Century Roman Baroque. Her book *Lives of the Most Eminent Painters* is a selection from Giorgio Vasari's classic biographies.

Cover Illustration:

The *Mona Lisa* (also known as *La Gioconda*) is shown from a close up view of the painting (see pages 140-141).

End Papers:

Front: Drawing, *A Crowned Eagle Standing on a Globe and a Wolf Steering a Boat.*
Back: A sheet of studies from the Windsor Collection.

Contents

I

The Mists of Youth

The quintessence of Leonardo is in this drawing, made in his old age when perhaps he sensed death peering over his shoulder. Wraithlike, half-smiling and mysteriously pointing, the woman sums up all the strange magic of the artist.

Sketch of a young woman pointing (enlarged), c. 1513

In one of the lion-colored stone houses in the town of Vinci in the Tuscan hills there was born on April 15, 1452, the most complex genius of the Renaissance and perhaps of all time: Leonardo. A searcher after unfathomable things, a painter of disquieting smiles that suggest the riddles of human personality, and of hands that point to mysteries beyond the earth, he seemed to his contemporaries a sort of magician, and to men in later centuries an Italian Faust.

The enigma of Leonardo begins with his birth. He was the illegitimate child of a woman about whom almost nothing is known—neither her surname nor her age, appearance, intelligence or education. As a rule biographers call her a peasant girl and let it go at that; in Vinci the tradition is that she was a barmaid. She is known only as Caterina. Of Leonardo's father, Piero da Vinci, there is a good deal more information but not enough for a clear picture. He was a notary and came from a family that had been established in Vinci at least as early as the 13th Century. His forebears for four generations had also been notaries, thrifty and shrewd enough to become upper middle-class landholders bearing the title of *Ser,* which fell also to Leonardo's father.

Ser Piero, who was in his mid-twenties at the time of his son's birth, was a man of impressive virility: he lived to be 77, had four wives (three died, one survived) and sired 12 children, the last when he was 75. He must also have been a capable notary—when, in his thirties, he moved a short distance down through the hills and established himself in Florence, his services were much in demand by the aristocrats of the city. But there is scant record of what he was like as a human being; if he had any talent or interest in the arts, that is unknown today.

Bastardy carried small stigma during the Renaissance. Illegitimate children emerged in households high and low, and frequently were recognized and treated equally with those born in wedlock. Alexander VI, the Borgia Pope, dandled at least four bastards of his own on the ecclesiastical knee. In that climate Leonardo was duly acknowledged by his father, even baptized in his presence and that of several other members of the family. He was not, however, taken immediately into the household. Soon after his birth he was sent, with Caterina, to a peasant's home in the nearby village of Anchiano. He remained there for perhaps four years, during which Ser Piero married the first of his series of wives, a 16-year-old girl of higher social standing than Leonardo's mother.

The young wife was barren. Possibly for that reason Leonardo was admitted to the Vinci house, to live with his grandparents, uncle, father and stepmother, at some time before he was five. The tax records for 1457 locate him there as *figlio di Piero illegittimo*. His boyhood in Vinci is a blank. In later years he was engrossed in botany, geology, the flight of birds, the character of sunlight and shadow and the motion of water, which suggests what he observed when he was young and spending much of his time roaming the countryside. That countryside, which has changed little in 500 years, is one of the most beautiful in Italy. Vinci is perched on a slope of Monte Albano, which in one direction descends toward the valley of the Arno and the city of Florence, and in another rises toward craggy, beckoning heights where there are great rocks, caves, and cold, darting little streams. Wherever the land is flat enough for cultivation there are small fields and vineyards where bent-backed men and women work with mattocks. Ancient olive trees, pruned into the shapes of stubby wineglasses so they may catch the sun in their bowls, stand in ranks or singly along the hills. Scattered roundabout are flowering almonds, and among them cypresses which resemble in form, if not in their green-black color, the brushes of enormous foxes. The air is so clear that from the heights of Monte Albano one can see the Mediterranean 40 miles away.

In the more than 7,000 pages of Leonardo's notes and drawings that survive there are no personal comments about his youth, and exceedingly few personal comments on any subject whatever. Once, in a theoretical passage on the formation of rivers, he set down the name of his childhood home, Anchiano—and then struck it out.

His education was that of any boy of good family in a small town: reading, writing, the elements of mathematics and Latin. He never got a good grasp of the latter and was obliged to struggle with it much of his life; many of the books available to him were in that language, although the Renaissance gave impetus to the use of Italian in literature and much had been published in the native language by the time of his death. He was sensitive about his lack of formal, humanistic education and later felt obliged to defend himself against unnamed critics who held that he was not "a scholar." His handwriting is extraordinary. It runs from right to left across the page and its letters are reversed, so that it can best be read with the aid of a mirror. There are various notions as to why he wrote thus, among them that he wished to protect his scientific ideas from the glance of the curious, and that he was a heretic who feared that accusations might be brought against him if his opinions became known. But in fact Leonardo was no more heretical than many another man of his time, and far from wishing to hide his scientific ideas, he intended eventually to publish them. The most logical explanation of his handwriting is that he was left-handed and found it convenient to write in that fashion. When it was necessary, as in marking names and directions on maps for others to read, he wrote in the usual way.

In one of the oldest accounts of Leonardo's life there appears a story that gives at least some insight into his youthful personality. It has the sound of truth because it strongly suggests the qualities he was known to have: extraordinarily keen observation, imagination and the ability to detach himself from the world around him. In the story, Leonardo's father is approached by a peasant of his estate who has cut a round shield from the wood of a fig tree and who asks Ser Piero to take it to Florence so that an artist may paint something on it. Ser Piero was indebted to the peasant for his skill in catching birds and fish, and so agreed. But instead of giving the shield to an established craftsman he gave it to Leonardo, who thereupon "began to think what he should paint on it, and resolved to do the head of Medusa to terrify all beholders. To a room to which he alone had access, Leonardo took lizards, newts, maggots, snakes, moths, locusts, bats and other animals of the kind, out of which he composed a horrible and terrible monster, of poisonous breath, issuing from a dark and broken rock, belching poison from its open throat, fire from its eyes and smoke from its nostrils. . . . He was so engrossed with the work that he did not notice the terrible stench of the dead animals, being absorbed in his love for art."

In time Ser Piero forgot about the shield, but when Leonardo had finished his painting he showed it suddenly, without warning, to his father, who was so startled that he began to run out of the room. "Leonardo detained him," says the story, "and said, 'This work is as I wanted it to be; take it away, then, as it is producing the effect intended.'

"Ser Piero indeed thought it almost a miracle," the story concludes, "and he warmly praised Leonardo's idea. He then quietly went and bought another round panel with a heart transfixed by a dart painted upon it, and gave it to the peasant, who was grateful to Piero all his life. Piero took Leonardo's work secretly to Florence and sold it to some merchants for one hundred ducats."

The story does not mention what Ser Piero did with the hundred ducats, leaving the implication that all Leonardo received for his efforts was warm praise. Father and son apparently were not close; many years later when the old man died Leonardo made only the briefest mention of the fact in one of his notebooks, commingled with observations on scientific matters. "On the 9th of July, 1504, Wednesday at 7 o'clock, died Ser Piero da Vinci, notary at the palace of the *Podestà* [governor], my father, at 7 o'clock. He was 80 years old, left ten sons and two daughters." The impersonality of the notice has an added chill because Leonardo appears to have jotted it down absentmindedly—he repeats "7 o'clock" and overstates his father's age by three years.

Whatever their relationship, Ser Piero recognized his son's talent, and when the boy was about 15 took him to Florence and allowed him to become apprenticed in an artist's studio. There is no description of Leonardo dating from that time, but not long after his death there appeared a few short biographies written by men who were his contemporaries, or nearly enough so that from them a fair idea of his charm can be derived. The most detailed work is that of Giorgio Vasari, the artist who was at the same time the first modern historian of art. Vasari could not have known Leonardo; the first printed edition of his *Lives of the Painters, Sculptors and Architects* appeared in 1550, 31 years after Leonardo's death, by which time the great man had become a legend. However, Vasari was a tireless researcher who sought out men who had been Leonardo's pupils and acquaintances, and came as close to the truth as he could. He describes Leonardo as a young man, not an apprentice boy, but the one could not have been greatly different from the other.

"Men saw this [the gift of God] in Leonardo da Vinci," Vasari wrote, "whose personal beauty could not be exaggerated, whose every movement was grace itself and whose abilities were so extraordinary that he could readily solve every difficulty." His strength was such, Vasari added, that "with his right hand he could bend the clapper of a knocker or a horseshoe as if they had been of lead"; as for temperament, the biographer ascribed to Leonardo "a spirit and courage invariably royal and magnanimous." Although no portrait of him as a young man is known to exist, he is described as being, like many Tuscans, tall, of fair complexion, with auburn hair.

Vasari notes that Leonardo "could sing and improvise divinely" upon the lyre—the association of music and the visual arts was very close during the Renaissance. Leonardo's "charming conversation won all hearts, and although he possessed nothing and worked little, he kept servants, and horses of which he was very fond, and indeed he loved all animals. . . . Often, when passing places where birds were sold, he would let them out of their cages and having paid the vendor the price asked, he let them fly away into the air, restoring to them their lost liberty." Leonardo's love of animals is evident in his scores of drawings of them; a letter written by a Florentine acquaintance suggests that this love led Leonardo to become a vegetarian. He was also fond of fine clothes, of tricks and practical jokes. According to Vasari, "he would often dry and clean the guts of a bullock and make them so small that they might be held in the palm of the hand. In another room he kept a pair of smith's bellows, and with these he would blow out one of the guts until it filled the room, which was a large one, forcing anyone there to take refuge in a corner."

Vasari's picture is that of a gregarious young man, singer, lute player, delightful in conversation. He could not have known what thoughts were forming in the young man's mind. "If you are alone you belong entirely to yourself," Leonardo later wrote. "If you are accompanied by even one companion you belong only half to yourself, or even less, in proportion to the thoughtlessness of his conduct; and if you have more than one companion you will fall more deeply into the same plight." There is nothing misanthropic in that idea; the converse of it has been the ruin of many men of genius—Oscar Wilde, for example—who dissipated their art in conversation. The face Leonardo presented to the world was an affable mask; at heart he was the most solitary of men.

Vasari made little reference to the life of the workshops and the artistic milieu of Florence in his biography of Leonardo. Ordinarily boys were apprenticed to masters at 14 or thereabouts, and served an average of six years before they were admitted to the painters' guild—St. Luke's

—and permitted to set up shop for themselves. Florentines had more respect for artists than had the citizens of other Italian city-states. Giotto, Leonardo's predecessor by 185 years, had been held in high regard, and as early as 1400 the Florentine writer Filippo Villani had argued that the fine arts deserved equal rank with "liberal" arts such as mathematics and philosophy.

But the medieval concept of the artist as a mere craftsman had not yet been completely broken down by the time of Leonardo's apprenticeship. It was unusual for members of the upper class to take up art other than as a pastime. Among Leonardo's contemporaries, or near-contemporaries, in the workshops were Sandro Botticelli, Antonio del Pollaiuolo, Fra Bartolommeo and Andrea del Sarto, the sons, respectively, of a tanner, a poulterer, a muleteer and a tailor. That they later achieved recognition and honor is a tribute both to the breadth of public vision and to the artists themselves. Leonardo, as much as any man of his time, helped to hasten the change in status. His works, his personality and his intellect were overawing; it became as inappropriate to speak of him as a craftsman as it might be, today, to speak of the sculptors Giacometti, Calder and Manzù as blacksmiths.

I t was to Andrea del Verrocchio, one of the most sought-after artists in Italy, that Leonardo was apprenticed. Although he has had the misfortune to be overshadowed as a painter by his pupil, Verrocchio was a man of great talent and unsurpassed versatility, a superb sculptor and bronze-caster, a skilled worker in precious metals and jewels, and a designer of costumes, pageants and banners. Commissions in all of these areas came into Verrocchio's large shop while Leonardo was there: busts and painted portraits of Florentine citizens; an Annunciation, a Baptism, various Madonnas; an ornate sarcophagus for the Medici; the bronze *David,* the *Doubting Thomas* and the *Boy with Dolphin* which stand today in Florence, as well as the powerful equestrian statue of Colleoni in Venice. The shop also handled the casting and lifting into place of the huge copper ball and cross on the dome of the Florentine cathedral, and the complete production of elaborate court festivities to honor the visit of Galeazzo Maria Sforza, Duke of Milan, to the city. Verrocchio, as Vasari says, "was never unoccupied. He was always at work on some sculpture or painting; he went frequently from one work to another so as not to become stale."

The relationship between Leonardo and Verrocchio was apparently cordial, although Leonardo never mentioned his master in his notebooks. He lived in Verrocchio's house, and even after he was admitted to the guild of St. Luke's in 1472, when he was 20, he continued to live there instead of striking out on his own. As an apprentice Leonardo doubtless followed the standard routine, commencing with the grinding of colors and other drudgery and then, as his skills increased, gradually being allowed to execute the simpler parts of whatever work Verrocchio happened to have in hand. Much of what he learned must have come directly from the master himself, but there were more advanced pupils or assistants in the shop, notably Pietro Perugino, six years older than Leonardo, from whom he may have learned basic techniques. In his turn Leonardo obviously

Leonardo's interest in nature expressed itself throughout his lifetime in renderings that combine the scientist's powers of precise observation with the artist's genius for conveying the vitality of growth. Here, he has drawn in red chalk, pen and ink the flowers and ribbony leaves of a star-of-Bethlehem; at left, lightly drawn, are the leaves of a crowfoot, and at right a wood anemone. Below are seeds and blossoms of a spurge.

helped and influenced younger apprentices such as Lorenzo di Credi, whose style eventually became so slavishly Leonardesque that it sometimes requires an expert eye to tell their works apart.

Near Verrocchio's shop was the rival studio of Antonio del Pollaiuolo, whose drawing *Battle of Ten Naked Men* suggests that Pollaiuolo was among the first of Renaissance artists to dissect corpses to study muscular structure. In all likelihood Leonardo frequently visited Pollaiuolo's shop to observe what was in progress. He was in contact, too, with men such as Botticelli and Alesso Baldovinetti as they moved about a city in intellectual ferment where art was debated on the street corners.

Everywhere, Leonardo could see the work of his predecessors; by walking only a short distance he could study the frescoes of Masaccio, the first great painter of the Early Renaissance, and close at hand were those of more recent artists—Paolo Uccello, Fra Filippo Lippi and Andrea del Castagno, on whose *Last Supper* Leonardo must have fixed his eyes in a long and critical stare. Nearby were the sculptures and reliefs of Donatello and Ghiberti. These men had not only made great advances in naturalism—through investigation of anatomy and emotional expression—but had brought a fresh approach to the old forms of religious subject matter. It was on the structure erected by them that Leonardo and such others as Michelangelo, Bramante, Giorgione, Raphael and Titian would one day build the shimmering spire of the High Renaissance.

The architecture of Florence must also have served as a school for Leonardo. At the time of his arrival in the city, the Baptistery, Giotto's tower and the body of the cathedral had long since been completed, but the Foundling Hospital, the Pazzi Chapel and the cathedral dome stood as imposing models of the new style. The Medici Palace and the Rucellai Palace were of recent construction, and the façade of Santa Maria Novella, the apse of Santissima Annunziata and the enormous Pitti Palace were still in scaffolding, along which a student might walk to see their inner workings laid bare.

As to actual textbooks, apprentices had but few, notably *The Craftsman's Handbook* written by Cennino Cennini sometime before 1437. It is concerned almost entirely with practicalities, the kind of tasks Leonardo must have performed, although its opening chapter contains a view of art that doubtless stuck in his mind, for years later he restated it in his own writings: "this is an occupation known as painting, which calls for imagination, and skill of hand, in order to discover things not seen, hiding themselves under the shadow of natural objects, and to fix them with the hand, presenting to plain sight what does not actually exist." Cennini's chapter headings sum up the nature of the book: "How to draw on several kinds of panels; How to make various sorts of black; How to keep miniver tails [used in making brushes] from getting motheaten." He devotes much space to the technique of fresco, explaining that a painter must wet down and plaster only so much of a wall as he thinks he can paint in a single day, for changes cannot be made on the next. It was this limitation that turned Leonardo's mind toward experiments in other mediums for wall painting—he drew immediate inspiration from the act of creating, and it was intolerable to him not to be able to make alterations whenever he wished. His later experiments sometimes led to magnificent effects, but sometimes to disaster.

Art theory, with one great exception, was not available in written form to apprentices of Leonardo's day; they acquired it by word of mouth and observation. Fifty years earlier the architect Filippo Brunelleschi had revolutionized art by working out the principles of linear perspective, by which the areas within the frames of paintings or reliefs become illusionistic extensions of real space: the effect of depth is achieved by the use of lines converging on a central vanishing point. After Brunelleschi's discoveries, quickly taken up by Donatello, Masaccio and Ghiberti, it was only by exception that art appeared flat and two-dimensional. But as far as is known Brunelleschi wrote no treatise; that task, the first of its kind undertaken since ancient times and one of the great achievements of the Renaissance, fell to the scholar and architect Leon Battista Alberti.

Alberti raised Brunelleschi's ideas to the level of scientific theory, producing treatises on painting, sculpture and architecture with which Leonardo surely was familiar. It was Alberti's thesis that besides acquiring the necessary technical skill, the "modern artist" should master geometry, optics and perspective; he must also understand the mechanisms of the human body, because "the movements of the body" reveal "the movements of the soul." Alberti was concerned particularly with the relationship between mathematics and art: the laws that govern the former must also apply to proportions in art. Certain ratios, he felt, found everywhere in the universe must indicate divine intent. It was thus no accident that Leonardo was fascinated by mathematics, applied it to his paintings and for many years thought it contained the key to all knowledge.

There were men in Florence in the 1460s and 1470s, other than artists, who had influence in shaping Leonardo's mind. One of these was Benedetto dell' Abbaco, a formidable scholar interested in commerce, mechanics and engineering. Benedetto's ideas may have turned Leonardo toward his lifelong interest in inventions and gadgets. As Vasari wrote, Leonardo "was the first, although a mere youth, that put forward the project of reducing the River Arno to a navigable channel from Pisa to Florence. He made designs for flour mills, fulling mills and machines which might be driven by the force of water."

Another man of stature was Paolo del Pozzo Toscanelli, an eminent scholar in mathematics, astronomy and medicine who had also become a geographer of distinction by studying books and charts and analyzing the accounts of travelers. Toscanelli believed that the Orient could be reached by sailing westward across the Atlantic; in 1474, a full 18 years before Columbus set out on his voyage, Toscanelli sent him a map and a letter urging him to make the attempt.

How much contact Leonardo had with such men it is impossible to say, but it is likely that he sought them out. He was direct and uninhibited in his search for knowledge; if someone possessed information of interest to him, he went straight to the source and asked for it. "Let Maestro Luca show you how to multiply roots," he reminded himself in a note, or, "Get the friar of the Brera to show you the *De Ponderibus*."

In the political life of Florence Leonardo had no part and apparently

A gypsy captain named Scaramuccia, whose likeness this may be, was one of many models, witting or unwitting, whose striking faces filled pages in Leonardo's notebooks. Grotesque faces particularly fascinated him: his renditions of them are not caricatures, as they express no irony; they are beauty's obverse, equally worthy of attention and definition.

no interest. Nominally a republic, Florence was in effect ruled by the family of the Medici and the circle of aristocrats and intellectuals who surrounded them. The principal instrument of power was the Medici bank, into which the wealth of the city, stemming from the manufacture and processing of silks and woolens, jewelry and fine cabinet work, was funneled. The Medici were patrons of art, but not of the individual artist Leonardo. Possibly they were disconcerted by the reputation that he had obtained even as a young man, and which was to grow stronger as he aged: brilliant, many-sided, but dilatory and undependable, likely to leave work half-finished. For his part, Leonardo could not have been at ease in the Medici court. As Neoplatonic humanists the Medici were deeply interested in classical antiquity. So too was Leonardo but not in the same antiquarian sense. They fancied themselves as latter-day Romans, sometimes affected the wearing of togas and addressed each other in polished Latin, which Leonardo, weak as he was in the language, may have found a bit ridiculous. At any rate, the rulers of Florence did little for him.

Apart from his artistic chronology, there are very few fixed dates that can be used to pinpoint Leonardo's activities in the decade of his twenties. One document, of April 8, 1476, when Leonardo was nearly 24, may or may not have some significance in his personal history, but it has loomed large in later analyses of him and cannot easily be overlooked. The Florentine rulers, as one means of holding power, maintained a box called the *tamburo* outside the Palazzo Vecchio, or town hall. Into this box one could drop anonymous accusations, which were investigated if and when witnesses came forward to testify before the police. On the date in question, the *tamburo* was found to contain a charge that Leonardo and three other young men had engaged in homosexual acts with a 17-year-old artist's model named Jacopo Saltarelli. The charge may have been motivated merely by spite; the accuser was never identified, no witnesses presented themselves and although the case went to court a second time two months later, it ultimately came to nothing. Today, one's inclination is to ignore the whole affair. But the circumstances of Leonardo's life, his comments on sex and his attitude toward women will not quite permit this. The charges will come again to mind.

Some time after this, probably in the years from 1476 to 1478, Leonardo set up his own studio. It is unknown when or where in Florence this was, but the fact that he was no longer working for Verrocchio is established by his acceptance of at least two independent commissions.

Another of the bits of paper that fix Leonardo in a certain place on a certain day is not a dated document but a small drawing. Although the sheet is useful to scholars because it indicates his style and his handwriting of the time, it is of no great consequence as art, and fits more properly into biography. It was Leonardo's habit, as Vasari records, to wander through the streets in search of beautiful or ugly faces; the ugly, to Leonardo, was not to be avoided but to be searched out as a variation of the beautiful. He was "so delighted when he saw curious heads, whether bearded or hairy, that he would follow anyone who had thus attracted his attention for a whole day, acquiring such a clear idea of him that when he went home he would draw the head as well as if the man had been present."

Leonardo did not commit all his impressions to memory but carried a sketchpad with him wherever he went, as he advises others to do in his great *Treatise on Painting:* "You should often amuse yourself when you take a walk for recreation, in watching and taking note of the attitudes and actions of men as they talk and dispute, or laugh or come to blows with one another . . . noting these down with rapid strokes, in a little pocket-book which you ought always to carry with you. And let this be of tinted paper, so that you cannot rub out, but must go on to the next page, for these are not things to be rubbed out but preserved with the utmost diligence; for there is such an infinite number of forms and actions of things that the memory is incapable of preserving them, and therefore you should keep those sketches as your patterns and teachers." The passage may well account for the relatively large number of Leonardo's drawings that survive; he rarely threw one away.

On December 28, 1479, Leonardo must have been walking in Florence with his sketchpad; he was then a few months less than 28. The date is fixed by a historical event. A year earlier there had occurred a bloody, unsuccessful conspiracy against the Medici, led by members of the Pazzi family; now one of the conspirators, who had fled to Turkey, had been dragged back to Florence by the long arm of the Medici and hanged from a public building. Leonardo saw the body, in that combination of pathos, dignity and outrage that the dead convey, and made a sketch of it. On the same sheet he made this note: "Small cap tan-colored, doublet of black satin, black-lined jerkin, blue coat lined with black and white stripes of velvet. Bernardo di Bandino Baroncelli. Black hose."

There are two views of Leonardo's stark words. One is that they suggest a horrifying and abnormal detachment from humanity: might he not, even in a single, brief phrase, have indicated revulsion or compassion or any emotion? The other view is that he was at that moment functioning as any artist must, making notes for a painting or more detailed drawing which he later hoped to execute, and into which he might have put his personal feelings.

No one can say. His personality is shrouded in mist, as are the first 30 years of his life, illuminated only by Vasari and such documentary fragments as the foregoing. The art that he produced is a far better gauge of the man. In 1481, when Leonardo was 29, there took place an event that must have galled if not humiliated him. Pope Sixtus IV, no doubt after consultation with the Medici, summoned the "best" Tuscan artists to work in the Vatican. Botticelli was called, as were Ghirlandaio, Signorelli, Perugino, Pintoricchio and Cosimo Rosselli—but not Leonardo. He cannot have escaped the feeling that Florence under the Medici held little future for him. He turned his eyes toward northern Italy, seeking the patronage of the powerful Lodovico Sforza, in whose court there was a more dynamic and less preciously intellectual atmosphere. In 1482 he went to Milan, beginning a separation from Tuscany that was to last almost 20 years, during which he would find the recognition he had not obtained at home.

The World He Knew

Time has dealt gently with the world of Leonardo. Were he now to stand as once he did, looking down across an olive grove at Vinci sleeping in the sun, his view would be essentially the same as it was 500 years ago. In two senses this image suggests flight: the act of soaring above the towers and over the distant hills, and the idea of escaping from a small town that, for all its loveliness, could be only a prison for him.

In his childhood the attraction of Florence, less than a day's journey distant, was no doubt overwhelming. In Vinci, Leonardo might see peasants whittling sticks, chipping stones or making such coarse fabrics as they wore —but the "City of Flowers" teemed with artists and with artisans, daily producing hundreds of shop and studio objects that to a boy must have seemed almost miraculous: tapestries, paintings, illuminated manuscripts, jewelwork, sculpture, decorated chests, cloth of the most exquisite texture and color.

The transition—or the flight—from Vinci to Florence was a radical one. Leonardo himself, in his thousands of pages of manuscript, never made the slightest reference to it, either in terms of melancholy at forsaking his childhood or joy at his liberation. To sense the explosive change from one environment to another, look long at the isolated little hill town of Vinci and then abruptly turn the page to bustling Florence.

In Leonardo's birthplace today, the two towers of Vinci stand like chess pieces in eternal confrontation. The square structure is a small castello, now a Leonardo museum. Facing it is the spire of the church in which, local tradition says, he was baptized.

In panorama the Florence of today is little different from the city of the 1460s. The Ponte Vecchio *(right)*, built over the River Arno in 1345, was lined with goldsmiths' shops in Leonardo's time and is still a center of the jewelry trade. The three tallest structures on the skyline are the crenellated tower of the Palazzo Vecchio, the bell tower designed by Giotto and the cathedral *(below)*. On the tip of the lantern above the dome may faintly be seen the gilded copper ball, seven feet six inches in diameter, placed there in 1471 by Verrocchio while Leonardo the apprentice looked on. The cathedral dominates the city both physically and in spirit: Florentines in Leonardo's time, wandering in alien lands, sometimes expressed their loneliness and nostalgia by saying that they suffered from "cathedral sickness"—*la malattia del duomo.*

Miniature from the 15th Century manuscript *De Sphaera*

The beauty of Florence stemmed not only from her great artists but from the thousands of highly skilled craftsmen whose names are forgotten. The exterior of the Duomo *(opposite),* intricately inlaid with white, green and pink marble, is an enduring testament to the talent of the anonymous stonecutters who worked on it. Other craft specialties may be seen above in a page from an illuminated manuscript—the copyist, with subtle pride, places his own profession in the spot first sought by the eye: upper left. Beneath him are clockmakers and armorers, and on the right in descending order may be seen a painter working on a triptych, a sculptor carving a statue, probably of wood, and a maker of pipe organs blowing into a metal tube to ascertain its pitch.

Sketch of the hanged Baroncelli (enlarged), 1479

In matching grimness, here are Leonardo's sketch of the anti-Medici conspirator, Bernardo di Bandino Baroncelli, and a photograph of the stark façade of the magistrate's palace from which he was hanged. The treacherous plot, conceived by members of the Pazzi family, may seem singularly outrageous to the modern mind—the assassins attacked Giuliano de' Medici and his brother, Lorenzo the Magnificent, while they were at worship in the cathedral. Moreover, they chose the most solemn moment of the service, the elevation of the Host, as the signal to draw their daggers and strike. Giuliano was killed on the spot, but the primary target, Lorenzo, escaped with only a minor wound. In the bloody aftermath, supporters of the Medici hunted down scores of Florentine citizens suspected of complicity and butchered them or put them to the noose.

Whatever one may think of the affair today, it is more appropriately viewed in Renaissance terms—and in the context of Leonardo's fellow men. The Tuscan citizen, shrewd, humorous, ferocious, was capable of conceiving and committing an infinitude of gross or subtle sins; but he had many redeeming traits, among them that he was not a hypocrite and despised a fool. To be sure, many Florentines were appalled at the monstrous act, but many others found it disgraceful for another reason: the conspiracy failed. After all, the Tuscan reasoning went, if one is to construct so elaborate and consequential a plot, one ought at least to be efficient and see that it succeeds. Such attitudes and events were integral to Leonardo's world; against that background his gentleness, reverence for life and hatred of dissembling were all the more remarkable.

II

Beginning
with an Angel

Leonardo's unfinished *St. Jerome* states one of his repeated themes: emotion reciprocated by man and animal. A seldom-noticed detail, the strange architectural apparition in the cleft in the rocks at upper right, hints at the material world from which the saint has withdrawn.

St. Jerome, c. 1481

Although Leonardo's undying reputation is rooted in other things as well as his art, it is nonetheless surprising that in his 67 years he produced so few paintings—little more than a dozen. And only in the past half century, because of advances in scientific techniques and historical analysis, have critics been able to reach some agreement as to what paintings are genuine Leonardos and to disqualify others, long attributed to him, that are merely Leonardesque.

One of the problems in detecting Leonardo's works lies in his own evolution as an artist: his High Renaissance masterpieces are so overpowering that it is difficult to accept his earlier paintings as coming from the same hand. Another difficulty stems from his influence, which he exerted not only through the relatively small number of his paintings but through intellectual stimulation, with the result that enough imitative works have been produced down through the centuries to fill a large gallery. A third problem arises from the collaborative custom of his time; he contributed portions to the paintings of his master, Verrocchio, and later, when he had his own pupils, they worked on Leonardo's compositions. In such joint efforts it is not always easy to distinguish Leonardo's hand. Walter Pater, a 19th Century interpreter of Renaissance art and literature, wrote one of the most beautiful and widely read studies of Leonardo less than a century ago—but today his work must be approached with care: through no fault of Pater's, many of the paintings discussed are not by Leonardo at all.

Fortunately, at the edge of this thicket Leonardo's earliest painting stands out beyond all question. Vasari writes specifically about it in his *Lives:* "Leonardo was placed, as I have said, with Andrea del Verrocchio in his childhood by Ser Piero, and his master happened to be painting a picture of St. John baptizing Christ. For this Leonardo did an angel holding some garments; and, although quite young, he made it far better than the figures of Andrea. The latter would never afterward touch colors, chagrined that a child should know more than he." The story of the master who is surpassed by his pupil, and who then abandons painting in frustration, is an old chestnut in the history of art. But Vasari's version may reflect something of what actually happened at the time of the painting of the *Baptism*.

Of all his skills, Verrocchio probably took the least satisfaction in painting. At this he was an able master in the style of the third quarter of the Italian Quattrocento (15th Century): a painter of large, naturalistic figures in bright, sunlit colors. His definition of forms was somewhat flat and linear, and his backgrounds, in the manner of the time, were receding plains and rounded hills with formalized rocks and trees spotted here and there. It is unlikely that the emergence of a young genius in his shop would have distressed him; it strengthened the shop (which was, after all, Verrocchio & Co.). He may even have stopped painting happily, glad of the freedom to devote more time to his major talents in metalwork and sculpture. It is unlikely, too, that Leonardo painted the angel when he was a "child"—Verrocchio's *Baptism of Christ (pages 44-45),* which hangs today in the Uffizi Gallery in Florence, dates from about 1472, when Leonardo was 20. Nonetheless this youthful work, like the first statement of a theme in music, sets forth some of the possibilities he would later develop.

The pose of the little blue-robed figure is free and supple. The turning of the body and head, the bending of the knee and arms, suggest that the angel has just moved into this position and is about to assume another. He is deeply involved in the action of the painting, focusing all his attention on the sacrament; in contrast, the immediately adjacent angel by Verrocchio stares into space like a bored choirboy awaiting the end of a tedious sermon. In the face of Leonardo's angel can be seen the first suggestion of his ideal of human beauty, not yet completely plastic, faintly feminine, but with muffled outlines and the famous, barely perceptible smile. The rippling hair is a premonition of Leonardo's lifelong fascination with sinuous, coiling motion; the tuft of grass beside the angel's knee a reminder of his keen perception of nature.

But arresting though the angel is—"a space of sunlight in the cold, labored old picture," as Walter Pater called it—it is still the work of a young painter. As an apprentice Leonardo "often made figures in clay which he covered with a soft, worn linen dipped in clay, and then set himself to draw them with great patience." Such studies done with a brush on a prepared cloth surface were standard practice for apprentices in the Florentine workshops, and may account for the hard, somewhat static appearance of the angel's drapery.

In addition to the angel, Leonardo contributed much of the landscape for the *Baptism.* It is not in Verrocchio's style—its pools and mists, patches of sunlight and shadow, prefigure the magical and almost hallucinatory landscape of the *Mona Lisa.* The landscape and the angel are done in oil, a medium that had only lately been introduced to Italy from the north, while Verrocchio's parts of the picture are in the traditional egg tempera. The latter ensured a bright enamel-like surface, but demanded strict demarcation between one color and another. It was entirely in character for the young Leonardo, who was to become the most avant-garde and experimental painter of his time, to seize on oil while his master continued in the old way.

One of the chief advantages of oil was the possibility of nuances of effect, and Leonardo began to explore these in the background of the *Baptism.* There he uses aerial perspective, which is quite different from the mathematical, linear perspective of Brunelleschi. By dictionary definition, aerial perspective is the creation of depth in painting by the use of gradations in color and distinctness; to Leonardo it was much more than that. He thought of air, atmosphere, as an almost palpable mass of particles floating between the eye and the objects it perceives—a transparent ocean in which all things exist and by which they are bound together. Air, full of light and humidity, haze and shadow, has a unifying function that brings foreground and background into relationship. Leonardo devoted years of his life and scores of pages of manuscript to studies of atmosphere and how to create the illusion of it in painting. His use of oil glazes to produce aerial perspective does not appear as very impressive in the dirty, overpainted and varnish-clouded background of the *Baptism,* but it is there, revealing his concern with it even at the beginning of his career.

Thus from the outset Leonardo regarded landscape not simply as a backdrop for studies of the human figure. He saw man in his whole environment, as an inextricable part of nature. Many years later, when he brought his early ideas to written form in his notes for his *Treatise on Painting,* he took to task no less a painter than Sandro Botticelli, who did not share his feeling for landscape. (It was extraordinary for Leonardo to reproach another artist by name. He avoided quarrels, and when he was abused by his young rival, Michelangelo, who hated him, he made no reply other than to note in his journal that it is wise to cultivate patience.) "He is not well rounded," wrote Leonardo, "who does not have an equally keen interest in all of the things within the compass of painting; for example, if someone does not delight in landscape, he therefore considers this to be a matter requiring only brief and rudimentary study. Thus, our Botticelli has declared this particular study to be vain, for if one but threw a sponge full of colors at the wall it would leave a patch in which one might see a beautiful landscape. It is probably true that one may see all sorts of things in such a patch—that is, if one wishes to look for them—such as human heads, different kinds of animals, battles, cliffs, the sea, clouds or forests, and other such things; it is just like the sound of bells in which you can imagine hearing whatever words you please. But even though such patches may help you to invent things, they will never teach you how to carry any particular project to completion. And that painter painted very sorry landscapes."

The point of Leonardo's swipe at Botticelli is plain enough: landscape is no trivial thing. But it is worth noting that he does not entirely dismiss the idea of studying a random, colored patch for the images which might appear in it. In another part of his *Treatise* he actually recommends staring at stains on walls as a source of inspiration; the 19th Century French author-painter Victor Hugo, following Leonardo, derived many of his ideas for drawings from the blots made by coffee stains on tablecloths.

Soon after his work on the *Baptism* Leonardo produced a drawing which has been called by Ludwig Heydenreich, the famed German scholar of Leonardo, "The first true landscape in art." Drawn with a pen, it shows a view from a height looking down into the valley of the Arno *(page 48).* It is made with quick, scurrying strokes that give it an Oriental flavor. Motion fills it, the rippling of water and the flutter of leaves; above all it reveals Leonardo, working directly from nature, as already a master of the effects of light and depth of atmosphere. It is one of the few drawings he ever saw fit to date—the inscription reads, "Day of St. Mary of the Snows, August 5, 1473." He may have dated it simply because he was young and full of pleasure in his burgeoning skill, but possibly he saw the drawing as something unique and wanted to leave no doubt as to when it was made.

After the landscape drawing and the precise, intimate glimpse of Leonardo it offers, the tangle of confusion concerning the rest of his early works grows dense. A rough consensus has been reached about some, but the debate about others will never end. Among Leonardo scholars, the best judgments are conceded to be those of Sir Kenneth Clark, former curator of the British Royal Collection and author of the classic study, *Leonardo da Vinci: An Account of His Development as an Artist.* In the labyrinthine arguments about authenticity it seems best to follow Clark's path.

The first painting in the early group is an *Annunciation,* now in the Uffizi Gallery in Florence *(pages 46-47).* It can be dated fairly accurately because of the lectern on which the somewhat startled Virgin rests her hand; it closely resembles the Medici sarcophagus now in the church of San Lorenzo, Florence, made in Verrocchio's shop about 1472, which Leonardo probably used as a model. The painting is not a great work of art nor has it been improved by the tampering of some later hand, which grossly enlarged the wings of the annunciatory angel. Originally modeled after the wings of a bird, they once were graceful and appropriate; now they seem grotesque. In the overall effect, however, can be seen some of Leonardo's predilections—a poised moment of human interaction, a profusion of growing things painted not as specimens or symbols but as a vital, energetic mass, and a vista at once clear and real, but somehow touched with wonder.

The portrait of *Ginevra de' Benci (page 49)* was probably painted from 1473 to 1474—it was the custom, then as now, for young ladies to have their portraits done at about the time of their weddings, and Ginevra's occurred in January 1474. The painting has been damaged, a piece having been cut off the bottom, which may have contained the lady's hands in a pose perhaps similar to that of the *Mona Lisa* some 30 years later.

Possibly Ginevra was cool by nature, or trapped for social or economic reasons in a loveless match, but it is hard to escape the feeling that Leonardo was not fond of her—or of women in general. The painting is distinguished by its melancholy mood and somber, twilit tones. The pallor of Ginevra's face is set in strong contrast to the darkness of the spiky foliage behind her (it is a juniper tree, for which an Italian dialect term is *ginevra*). The background is veiled in a thin mist, created with oil glazes laid one over the other, that softens outlines and blurs the forms.

The effect is called *sfumato* (literally, "turned to vapor"); though not invented by Leonardo, it was a technique of which he became the greatest master the world has known. The delicate haze that clings to and surrounds the shapes produces a dreamlike atmosphere through which the inmost nature of natural objects or of personality may be sensed more deeply than in the dry glare of noon.

After his painting of Ginevra, Leonardo entered a period of preoccupation with the theme of the Virgin and Child. From approximately 1476 to 1480, the 24th to 28th years of his life, he executed a series of such studies. Some survive as completed, if partly ruined, paintings, others only in sketches. Of the paintings, the *Virgin with Flowers,* now in Munich, and the *Litta Madonna* and the *Benois Madonna,* both in Leningrad, are in such poor condition that only details certify them as Leonardo's. Where time and the repainter's brush have left them intact, one can see bits of landscape, beautifully executed fragments of nature, hands, waves of hair, draperies, that could scarcely have been done by another.

Characteristics of Leonardo's early drawing style show clearly in this sketch of a unicorn purifying a pool of water with its horn. A few swelling strokes define the curving contours of the animal. The hatchings, or shading lines, creating the space around the form run downward from left to right, the natural path for the left-handed artist like Leonardo.

The preliminary drawings, which Leonardo always kept close beside him, for both these and for other Madonnas that were never completed as paintings, are of much greater interest. One such drawing, now at Windsor Castle in England, shows the Madonna and Child accompanied by the infant St. John, the earliest combination of these figures from Leonardo's hand. There is no Biblical evidence of any encounter between Christ and St. John as children—that was a medieval invention which had deep meaning for the artists of Florence, where John the Baptist is the patron saint. Although John appears in Leonardo's drawing with complete naturalness and not with any sense of mechanical device, the great Renaissance authority Bernard Berenson has pointed out that the addition of the saint gives precisely the balance to make the composition a pyramid. Leonardo would later greatly develop the pyramidal arrangement, which became a hallmark of High Renaissance artists and of Raphael in particular.

Among the other drawings are studies for the *Madonna and Child with a Cat* and a *Madonna and Child with a Plate of Fruit.* They—indeed all of Leonardo's drawings from this period—are full of a wonderful grace and spontaneity. His quickness of vision was superhuman; it has been said, and substantiated by analyses of his drawings of fast-moving water and the beating of birds' wings, that Leonardo observed details which were not analyzed again by man until the invention of the slow-motion camera. The swelling and diminishing of the lines themselves eliminated the need for much internal modeling. When he used shading, it was in firm, parallel hatching slanting down from left to right—the natural stroke of a left-handed artist. (In evaluating Renaissance drawings attributed to him, experts automatically look first at the shading; if it is not left to right, the strong presumption is that the work is not Leonardo's.) He rarely made a finished so-called "presentation" drawing during this period. The British Museum's sheet of an *Antique Warrior (page 33),* from around 1475, is one of the few examples known.

Leonardo's spontaneity and freedom of line raise a question: Why do they not carry over into the Madonna paintings which, even allowing for the leaden-handed reworking of later artists, must have been fairly heavy in the original? Sir Kenneth Clark, who puts the question, also answers it. There were two divisive traditions in the art of the Quattrocento. One, exemplified by Fra Filippo and Botticelli, involved fancy and grace of line; the other, to which Leonardo's master Verrocchio was committed, insisted on scientific naturalism. Leonardo's instincts placed him in the first group, but his training and intellect inclined him toward the second. Thus, between the freshness of his original inspiration and its final execution as a painting, a great deal of work intervened. He reduced his fanciful sketches to severe diagrams and highly finished studies of detail. "He might have been a prolific painter," as Clark says, "[but] by the time he began to paint, constant labors and anxieties had so deprived him of all appetite for his subject that his pictures were either left unfinished, or, as with the *Benois Madonna,* were carried through without that vitality, that spontaneous rendering of action, which was the original motive of the whole conception."

When Leonardo was not drawing with a purpose but simply doodling or warming up, he was in the lifelong habit of filling sheets with profile heads. He made scores of them, all more or less the same: a dour, even ferocious old man juxtaposed with a handsome, somewhat effeminate youth. The psychological meaning of these sketches has been much explored; one interpretation is that they represent the duality of Leonardo's nature. In the area of his art, they may also represent the confrontation of grace and imagination on one hand and the stern discipline of scientific naturalism on the other.

Leonardo's struggle to reconcile the conflicting forces within him can be seen in the innumerable studies and the incomplete painting of his first major work, the *Adoration of the Magi (pages 134-135).* The *Adoration* was intended to be an altarpiece for the monastery of San Donato a Scopeto, whose monks were clients of Leonardo's father. The monks eventually had some cause to regret the commission, as Leonardo never got beyond the underpainting, but if they had any prescience in art they may well have realized that the unfinished painting Leonardo left them was beyond price. It was revolutionary—the most dramatic, highly organized work of the Quattrocento, before which succeeding generations of artists would stand speechless in wonder.

In Renaissance art there had been many previous Adorations, both of magi and of shepherds; their common characteristic was narrative. But Leonardo chose to ignore narrative in order to portray the maelstrom of emotions that accompanied the most awesome event in the history of Christian man, the appearance on earth of the Son of God. He chose also to ignore the logic that would have dictated the presence only of rural folk or magi or both: he included the whole sweep of humanity in his picture. One critic has counted no fewer than 66 figures, among them youths and old men, poets and warriors, believers and doubters.

One of the first sketches for the *Adoration* is a drawing in the Louvre in which two of the final elements of the composition can be seen—the mass of figures around the Virgin and the crumbling architecture of the background *(page 129).* It is a tentative sketch, full of half-formed thoughts, even in the perspective. As he developed his ideas, Leonardo made a second pen drawing which is a Brunelleschian wonder, its straight lines creating so dominant a vanishing point at right center that one's instinct is to reach out and jab it with a forefinger *(page 134)*. The real fascination of the drawing lies not in its perfect linear perspective, however, but in the human and animal figures Leonardo put into it. They are, in the approving sense of the word as used by modern artists and musicians, "wild." In a scene of ruins there are horses, ridden by naked men, prancing, rearing, kicking. Naked figures crawl up the stairs, at the top of which, along a balcony, men and animals writhe in a fantastic tangle. At the left stands a man swinging some implement, apparently an ax, as though chopping down a column, and near him, for the first and only time in Leonardo's art, appears a camel. (The animal represents at least a small compromise with tradition; at this stage in his thinking he apparently wanted to suggest a Middle Eastern atmosphere. Where he may have seen a camel is a matter of guesswork. The Medici maintained a small zoo in Florence; perhaps he saw the animal there. In any case, he eliminated the camel when he began to paint.)

A product of Leonardo's apprentice years is this elaborate portrait of a warrior. While the identity of the subject is not certain, it may have been drawn after one of Verrocchio's bronze reliefs: it resembles his equestrian monument of *Colleoni (page 39)*.

Why should Leonardo have put these figures into his composition? One reason is that he deeply felt the relationship of all living things: trees, flowers, animals and men rolling together on this mysterious earth toward some unfathomable destiny. If a man may shout or cavort in exultation, may not a horse prance? His thought was not simple; he would have recoiled from the pat homily of Coleridge's *Ancient Mariner*—"He prayeth best, who lovest best/ All things both great and small;/ For the dear God who loveth us,/ He made and loveth all." But Leonardo did see a commonality of emotion between man and beast. His famous drawing of a horse, a lion and a man, side by side, all with their teeth bared in anger, is a sharp and disconcerting comment. However, it is presumptuous to analyze his motives. In all the arts, the test of a piece of imagination is whether or not it works; in the *Adoration*, it works.

The composition of the painting contains at its center the basic pyramid: its apex is the Virgin's head, with the right diagonal running down the extended arm of the Child and the back of a kneeling wise man to the ground. The left diagonal, less clearly defined, runs down the slope of the Virgin's shoulder and through the head of another prostrate man. Enclosing this pyramid is a turbulent arc of humanity, close-pressed, bending, gesturing in an incredible variety of expressive poses. The symbolism in the painting is hard to extract, so richly is it overlaid with personal visions. But it is still there: crumbling architecture was a long-established reference to the decay of paganism at the birth of Christ; and the palm, placed directly above the Virgin and Child, is the Tree of Life.

Setting aside the immense amount of thought and the many preparatory sketches for the *Adoration*, Leonardo worked on the painting for only seven months, not enough time for him to complete even the now dusky yellow and slate-colored groundwork. But in this unfinished state, perhaps even more than might be the case if he had finished it, the *Adoration* serves wonderfully to illustrate his technique of modeling in chiaroscuro, the contrast of light and dark. His great artistic concern was never with color or outline but with the creation of three-dimensional effects. "A painting impresses the spectator only when it makes that which is not real seem to be raised and detached from the background," he wrote. "The colors, however, only redound to the credit of the man who prepared them, for nothing about them save their beauty can be admired. . . . And something may be painted in ugly colors and still excite the admiration of the spectator because it seems plastic." And this chiaroscuro is technically the most striking feature of the *Adoration*. The figures seem to emerge and recede in the shadows, parts of them roundly modeled in the light and others dim but implied in the dusk. They do not stand side by side in Quattrocento style, but are part of a massive unit in which the boundaries between them fade away.

Of approximately the same date as the *Adoration* is a *St. Jerome (page 26)*, also unfinished, which has occupied a place of honor in the Vatican Gallery since 1845, although in earlier times, to judge by its present appearance, it must not have been held in much regard. Someone cut the wooden panel into two parts, one of which was used as a table top; the parts were discovered separately in Rome around 1820 by Joseph Cardinal Fesch, an uncle of Napoleon, who had them botchily reunited. Like the *Adoration,* the *St. Jerome* is skillfully modeled in chiaroscuro, probably originally in slates and white, which 19th Century varnish has turned to muted golds and olives. Leonardo shows the saint beating his breast with a stone in penitential passion. There is nothing venerable about the old man, bald and beardless, seated among rocks in a desert with a lion at his feet—the lion, its mouth open not in a roar but a howl, seems to share Jerome's suffering. (Jerome, like the Greek Androcles, is believed to have extracted a thorn from the foot of a lion that was ravaging the countryside around his monastery, and thus befriended the beast.) The saint's emaciated body has a fascinating complexity of movement; every limb is on a different axis. Lines extended downward from his tilted face, upward from his leg and horizontally from his left hand all converge on his chest at the point of impact of the stone.

The virile and the effeminate—two poles of Leonardo's nature—show up in recurrent drawings of two facing heads—often an old yet obviously once-powerful man and a soft-faced boy. The youth with ringleted hair shown here is probably Salai, the boy whom Leonardo took into his household in 1490.

Leonardo apparently was much possessed by St. Jerome as a subject. In a list of his works drawn up in about 1482 he set down "certain figures of St. Jerome," which suggests that there were several. Today, when few, save studious Catholics, are familiar with the long roster of saints, a brief note about the man may be relevant. Jerome, who lived around 340 to 420 A.D., was irritatingly outspoken and quarrelsome, but that was not the reason for his penitence. Like Leonardo, he was an intellectual with a very wide range of interest. It was he who revised the old Latin of the Gospels and translated the Old Testament from Hebrew into Latin, thus creating the Vulgate Bible. However, he was also deeply versed in the pagan literature of Greece and Rome—to narrowminded early Christians, it may have seemed that Jerome knew too much, or at least that he was interested in too many forbidden things. Jerome himself recorded a dream in which Christ reproached him for his interest in Cicero. The thirst for knowledge was Jerome's great temptation, as it was Leonardo's. In the painting Jerome appears to be trying to batter that temptation out of his soul. Self-flagellation and the denial of knowledge were anathema to Leonardo, who had great respect both for the body and for learning, but he may have felt kinship and compassion for a man in Jerome's plight.

There remains one more painting that may be placed stylistically among the works of Leonardo's early period. Exactly where it was painted is one of the touchiest subjects in recent scholarly debate, although it is generally agreed that it was not done before he left Florence in 1482, but soon after he arrived in Milan in that or the next year. The painting, the first of Leonardo's which has survived intact and in its original dimensions, is the Louvre version of the *Madonna of the Rocks (page 50)*. In it Leonardo at last succeeded in reconciling the worlds of imagination and scientific naturalism: the painting is a mysterious revelation with a setting that is not of this earth, a watery cave, open to the sky, sheltering the Virgin, the infants Christ and John and an angel. But the figures are supremely graceful and at ease, and the details of plant life are as true to nature as the most skilled botanical artist could draw them.

The *Madonna of the Rocks,* full of suggestions and symbols that lie just beyond the reach of the mind, reveals Leonardo at his most enigmatic. What is the meaning of the angel's emphatic gesture, aimed not at Christ but at John? Is the little figure, protected by the Virgin's hand and cloak, indeed John, or does he represent all of humanity in need of divine protection? Was the cave deliberately painted as a womblike enclosure suggesting the beginnings of life? Is it possible that Leonardo, a student of geology and biology, by some enormous, overleaping intuition, put into his painting the primordial ingredients—water, rock and sun? Scholars ruminate on such things; Leonardo himself, like most great painters, never made the slightest effort to explain this or any other of his works, trusting that other men too can sense things that lie beyond words.

At the center of the painting is perhaps the most wondrous interplay of hands in all art, protecting, worshiping, blessing, pointing. As the eye moves outward from these hands to study the entire picture, it becomes apparent that the painting is a summing up of all that Leonardo has learned. Aerial perspective is there, particularly in the landscape that may be seen through an opening in the rocks. The figures form the familiar pyramid, again with the head of the Virgin at its apex. In the face of the angel, Leonardo's ideal of beauty is finally realized, the features no longer drawn on the surface as in his angel for Verrocchio's *Baptism,* but built up from within. The cave is twilit, with a thin haze of *sfumato* in the moist air. The modeling of the figures in chiaroscuro is so fine that there seem to be no definite outlines; faces and bodies gently materialize as light strikes them; and the shadows in the rear of the cave are so dense that they appear to have substance. But it is not a dark picture—although layers of varnish have dimmed the colors, they still glow.

Whatever the meaning of the painting, and whenever or wherever it was done, there is one certainty about it. It was Leonardo's farewell to the Quattrocento; he had mastered and gone far beyond the art of the Early Renaissance. A number of years were to pass before he would undertake another painting of major caliber, but when at last he did, it would be a wonder of the world, the first classic statement of the ideals of the High Renaissance: the *Last Supper.*

Master and Pupil

Before turning to the works that survive from Leonardo's early Florentine years, one might well look first at the art of his contemporaries—notably that of his master Andrea del Verrocchio. Leonardo was apprenticed to Verrocchio as a teen-aged boy, and left no written comment about him except the oblique remark, "Poor is the pupil who does not surpass his master." Nonetheless, Leonardo owed his master a debt that extended well beyond the practical matters he learned in the studio. The remarkably versatile Verrocchio was the foremost sculptor of his day, and in his bronze *David (opposite)* may be seen some of the stylistic elements that Leonardo adopted, adapted and employed throughout his life. There, for example, are the curling, sinuous aureole of hair and the angelic face with its haunting half-smile. There, too, is the beautiful *contrapposto,* or counterpoise: the figure does not stand in unnatural stiffness but completely at ease, its body slightly twisted and its weight principally carried on its right or "engaged" leg.

No doubt Leonardo was instinctively inclined toward these things, and it may not have required any teacher to arouse his interest in them. Still, Andrea del Verrocchio employed them before Leonardo, and in watching his master create such stunningly graceful sculptures as the *David,* Leonardo learned to carry instinct to execution.

Verrocchio's *David,* slightly smaller than life-size, was produced when Leonardo was about 21. An old persistent story, repeated in various modern commentaries, has it that the face is a portrait of young Leonardo, but this is almost certainly romantic fiction.

Andrea del Verrocchio:
David, c. 1473

Attributed to Lorenzo di Credi: *Portrait of Verrocchio,* c. 1485

In this portrait attributed to Lorenzo di Credi, another of his pupils, one can sense the intelligence and strength that enabled Andrea del Verrocchio to excel in almost every art known to the Renaissance. When he sat for the portrait in about 1485, Verrocchio was already 50 years of age and at work on the last and greatest sculpture of his career—an equestrian monument *(opposite)* to the *condottiere* Bartolommeo Colleoni, which still stands today in Venice. The rider, his face set in "the sneer of cold command," as Shelley put it, barely touches the reins, seeming to control his mount only by the brute power of his will. The muscles of the horse's haunch and foreleg, tense with restrained energy, emerge in such a strong relief that the animal appears almost to have been flayed—testimony to Verrocchio's interest in the new science of anatomy which was burgeoning at that time. Verrocchio labored on his magnificent *Colleoni* statue for perhaps 10 years but he did not live to see it placed on its pedestal—he died in Venice when he was only 53. The casting of his masterpiece was finally completed by Alessandro Leopardi, who added certain decorative details and his own signature to the work.

Andrea del Verrocchio: *The Colleoni Monument,* 1479-1488

Andrea del Verrocchio:
Boy with Dolphin, c. 1475

SAGITTE TVE INFIXE SVNT MICHI

Pietro Perugino: *St. Sebastian*, c. 1500

Leonardo must also have learned much from Verrocchio's beautiful portrait bust of the *Lady with Primroses (opposite page)* and his fountain, *Boy with Dolphin (above)*. The *Lady* is the first bust in Renaissance art in which hands are shown, and in its slight twist of the head and the irregular fall of its drapery it departs from the tradition of formal frontality. The *Boy with Dolphin* is much more remarkable in its use of motion—the legs, head, wings and fish are all on different axes, creating the impression that the figure is about to pivot on its heel even as one looks at it.

Verrocchio's other pupils—Pietro Perugino, for example, whose *St. Sebastian* appears at right—were somewhat more conservative than the master. Although the atmosphere in Perugino's painting has a purity and freshness of unrivaled beauty, the slim, elegant body of the saint is motionless and the expression is blandly impersonal.

Andrea del Verrocchio: *Lady with Primroses*, c. 1478

Antonio del Pollaiuolo: *Rape of Deianira*, c. 1475

Alesso Baldovinetti: *Annunciation,* c. 1467

Among older, established Florentine masters whose works Leonardo knew well were Alesso Baldovinetti and Antonio del Pollaiuolo. The composition of Baldovinetti's *Annunciation,* a tempera panel shown at left, may have influenced Leonardo when he undertook his own version of the subject *(pages 46-47).* Probably of greater interest to him were Baldovinetti's experiments with traditional techniques to achieve richer pictorial effects. In Pollaiuolo's *Rape of Deianira* the landscape has a sweep and depth unknown before—the background, showing Florence in its valley, is not merely a stage setting but is integral to the work. The Hercules at right handsomely illustrates Pollaiuolo's pioneering studies in anatomy and the correct representation of the active human body.

The two saints immediately below, Ghirlandaio's *Jerome* at left and Botticelli's *Augustine,* suggest what men of Leonardo's own age, brought up in the same artistic milieu, had learned. Ghirlandaio's painting is precise and Botticelli's is expressive; in his *Augustine* the clutching hand and gnarled face are similar in feeling—though by no means in power—to the effects Leonardo achieved in his unfinished *St. Jerome (page 26).* But both the Ghirlandaio and the Botticelli belong unmistakably to the Quattrocento, an age that Leonardo soon transcended.

Domenico Ghirlandaio: *St. Jerome in His Study,* 1480

Sandro Botticelli: *St. Augustine in His Study,* 1480

Andrea del Verrocchio: *Baptism of Christ*, c. 1472

Although Verrocchio may have entrusted the youthful Leonardo with petty details of earlier works, it was apparently in the *Baptism of Christ* that he first allowed his apprentice to paint an entire figure. The little blue-robed angel, shown in its context at the far left of the entire painting and in detail on the opposite page, was in a sense Leonardo's notification to Florence that a great new genius was arising. Verrocchio, according to the art historian Vasari, was stunned, for he was faced with a premonition emanating from an unknown future world. Nor was it with the angel alone that Leonardo announced himself—he did so, as well, in the fragment of background isolated below, where misty, dreamlike depths foreshadow the wonders he would later create in *Mona Lisa* and the *Virgin and Child with St. Anne*.

Leonardo: landscape, detail from Verrocchio's *Baptism of Christ*

Leonardo: kneeling angel in profile, detail from Verrocchio's *Baptism of Christ*

The first painting produced wholly by Leonardo is the *Annunciation*
below, which dates from about 1472. Many critics are reluctant to credit
(or perhaps discredit) him with this work because of its awkward composition
and labored perspective, but it would have been well-nigh miraculous,
after all, if the artist at 20 or 21 had produced a masterpiece in his first attempt.
Other hands have tampered with it—the angel's wings, for example,
have been grotesquely enlarged—but the painting contains elements that
certify it as Leonardo's. The draperies are very similar to those he painted
in Verrocchio's *Baptism,* and among Leonardo's drawings there is an undoubted

study for the sleeve of the angel who appears in this work. Above all, the treatment of flowers and trees surpasses mere decoration and creates a sense of brooding wonder; as Sir Kenneth Clark observes, ". . . the black trees silhouetted against the grey evening sky are one of those effects which first, in our childhood, made us feel the poetry and, as it were, the closeness of nature." In the foreground the flowers are no perfunctory, space-filling arrangement of pretty little specimens, but a writhing, energy-filled mass that re-creates the vital, botanical world as it actually is, and as in Italy up to that time only the youthful Leonardo had painted it.

Annunciation, c. 1472

Arno Landscape, 1473

Leonardo's pen drawing of the valley of the Arno, dated in mirror script, "Day of St. Mary of the Snows, August 5, 1473," is the first Renaissance work that deals wholly with landscape. The drawing is discussed on page 30, but here one might profitably look at it first with eyes wide-open and then half-closed to see the quick, broken strokes merge into solidity and the atmosphere deepen and become oceanlike.

The first of Leonardo's painted portraits, that of Ginevra de' Benci on the opposite page, was probably begun in 1474, when he was 22. Even at that age he was preoccupied with chiaroscuro, as the strongly contrasted areas of light and shadow make plain. Formerly the only privately owned Leonardo painting, the work became the first in an American museum when the National Gallery in Washington bought it for a record five million dollars in the winter of 1967.

On the next pages are Leonardo's two great versions of the *Madonna of the Rocks.* The first shows how completely, at the age of about 31, he had mastered—and grown beyond—all he could learn from the art of the Quattrocento. The second, some 25 years later in date, belongs to the period in which he had become the first master of the High Renaissance.

Ginevra de' Benci, c. 1474

Madonna of the Rocks (Louvre version), c. 1483

Madonna of the Rocks (London version), c. 1506

III

The Master
in Milan

Leonardo's portrait of Cecilia
Gallerani, Sforza's mistress, shows her
holding an ermine, one of the Duke's
emblems. Since it has been partially
repainted, the authorship of the work
has been questioned; but Leonardo's
touch is undeniably evident in the
twisting pose of the animal and the
exquisite modeling of the lady's hand.

Lady with an Ermine, c. 1483

The ostensible reason given by early biographers for Leonardo's going to Milan in 1482, when he was 30, was that he went there to play the lute in the court of Lodovico Sforza. The instrument he took with him, for which a drawing still exists, he made of silver in the shape of a horse's skull. That strange device was typical of Leonardo's taste for the bizarre, but it was no mere gimcrack; the hollow of the skull gave the lute strong volume and resonance. Among other instruments of his design were a wheeled drum that beat rhythmically as it was pulled along, an automatic hammer and bell that struck one clear note at a time, and an organist viola, a device with a spring-driven bow used by beggars, in the manner of the hurdy-gurdy of recent memory. His interest in music, however, apparently did not extend to composition. His papers contain only one bit of notation, part of a canon.

Leonardo's actual reason for leaving Florence has already been suggested: he felt that Lodovico Sforza would be a better patron than the Medici. To establish himself with Sforza he wrote a remarkable letter, saying nothing of music and mentioning art almost as an afterthought. The principal subject he addressed himself to was quite different: among his various personalities, nested inside each other like a set of Chinese boxes, there was Leonardo, military expert and weaponeer.

"I have plans for bridges," he wrote, "very light and strong, and suitable for carrying very easily. . . . I have plans for destroying every fortress or other stronghold unless it has been founded upon rock. . . . I have also plans for making cannon, very convenient and easy of transport, with which to hurl small stones in the manner almost of hail. . . . I have ways of arriving at a certain fixed spot by caverns and secret winding passages, made without any noise even though it may be necessary to pass underneath trenches or a river. . . . I will make covered chariots, safe and unassailable, which, entering among the enemy with their artillery, there is no body of men so great but they would break them. . . . I can make cannon, mortars, and light ordnance, of very beautiful and useful shapes, quite different from those in common use. . . . I can supply catapults, mangonels, trebuchets and other machines of wonderful efficacy."

Following this catalogue, in two sentences, Leonardo noted that he was skilled in painting and sculpture and that he might undertake *The Horse,* an equestrian statue Sforza had in mind.

The letter was shrewdly calculated. Lodovico's regime was shaky—he had usurped power in Milan and as any intelligent job applicant might have surmised, he should have welcomed a designer of weapons. As it developed, he was not interested in Leonardo's military inventions. One may wonder how Leonardo had come by these ideas in the first place.

During the Renaissance it was common for artists to be familiar with weaponry—a man who could cast a bronze statue could with equal facility make a cannon. And since fortifications were a branch of architecture, it was easy to turn from the design of *palazzi* and chapels to turrets and bastions. Both Giotto and Michelangelo drew plans for the defenses of Florence. Moreover, Leonardo, in the endless search for knowledge that was at once his greatness and his tragedy, had studied the contemporary treatise of Roberto Valturio, *De Re Militari.*

Leonardo drew on other sources and on his own intellect for his ideas. His "covered chariots, safe and unassailable" had been crudely conceived in Roman times as wheeled structures, heavily roofed with timbers, that could be brought up against city walls to shield the operators of battering rams. Leonardo greatly refined this idea into a turtle-shaped armored car or tank, fitted with cannon, to be propelled by eight men within, using cranks and gears. It is doubtful that human muscle could have moved so heavy an object any appreciable distance, particularly over uneven terrain. In this, as in so many of his inventions, Leonardo was fascinated more by the concept than by its execution. After sketching his "tank" he went on to other ideas, leaving the problem of motive power to posterity.

From classical literature he derived the scheme of a chariot armed with scythes and improved it with a mechanism that rotated the blades horizontally. He made a horrendous drawing of it in action—but then noted that scythed chariots often did as much harm to those who used them as they did to the enemy. Among his ordnance "out of the common type" was a multibarreled cannon in which 36 guns were mounted in three tiers of 12; while one tier was being fired, the second was cooling and the third being loaded. There was nothing impractical about that; it was the forerunner of the machine gun and the multiple rocket-launcher. Leonardo also sketched a bombshell that would explode on impact, scattering metal fragments. Here his design seems workable; if the bombshells had been constructed, Leonardo's name might today be a common noun; the man who brought the idea to effective use, at the end of the 18th Century, was a British officer named Henry Shrapnel.

In approaching Sforza as a military expert, Leonardo took the right tack with the wrong man. He did not yet know Lodovico, who would not even deign to give him the opportunity to build the weapons and test them. Sforza, who was called *Il Moro* according to some scholars because he was swarthy, and according to others because the mulberry tree *(moro)* was one of his emblems, was a devious, cautious ruler who preferred intrigue to war. He was suspicious of innovators, particularly non-Milanese; he was close-fisted; and although people to whom he owed money or

This complicated musical instrument is a lute made from a horse's skull, with ram's horns attached, which Leonardo cast in silver and took as a gift from his Medici patron to Lodovico Sforza of Milan. The snout is at left, decorated to resemble a bird's head; the bony eye socket is at the center, the strings stretch across the roof of the mouth. The lute was turned upside down for playing.

who brought him news he did not wish to hear did not believe so, he was moderately intelligent. When pressed, *Il Moro* assumed a frustrating attitude of incomprehension; Leonardo would have experience of this.

In other regards Sforza had the usual array of vices to be expected of any Renaissance despot, with the exception that he may have killed only one of his relatives. That was his nephew Gian Galeazzo Sforza, who had a better claim to Milan than *Il Moro* and actually bore the title of Duke. Gian Galeazzo was nominally the ruler when Leonardo arrived, but he was only 12 and a weakling to boot. *Il Moro* utterly dominated him, even after he reached maturity. He "reigned" during much of Leonardo's stay in Milan, then died of what was said to be a poison provided by his uncle.

Milan under Sforza was immensely rich. Textiles provided some of its wealth, and the manufacture of arms the rest. The fertile plain of Lombardy amply provisioned the city of 100,000, and the life of the court was the most glittering in Italy. Sforza spent huge sums on jewels, pageants, armies of servants, grooms and cooks. He had a magnificent chorus of Flemish singers and a company of musicians from Germany. Magicians and astrologers wielded great influence—Lodovico's personal astrologer, Ambrogio da Rosate, had so great a reputation that even the Pope, Innocent VIII, asked him for a horoscope. (Leonardo despised superstition but seems not to have been free of curiosity in the matter; his notes contain occasional entries of expenditures "for fortune-telling.") The morality of the court was summed up thus by Corio, its historian: "Fathers sold their daughters, brothers their sisters and husbands their wives there."

To Leonardo, Lodovico must at first have seemed an ideal patron because of his lavish spending and his interest in art. However, it was not the interest of a connoisseur; Sforza, like many a *nouveau riche,* wanted art as a status symbol. The painters and sculptors of Milan lagged far behind those of Florence; in architecture, Milan had little of interest beyond its ancient Romanesque church of Sant'Ambrogio and its overly elaborate late Gothic cathedral, the largest in Italy. Thus Lodovico imported artists, among them Leonardo and the architect Bramante—but he was uncertain as to how to employ them and niggardly in his payments.

The first commission Sforza gave to Leonardo was *The Horse,* on which the the artist labored intermittently for 16 years. Sforza's interest in the horse is a good gauge of his position in Milan. The Sforza line had been established in the city for only two generations, Lodovico's father, a freelance general named Francesco, having taken power after the collapse of the Visconti rule. To consolidate his position, Lodovico hoped to erect a statue of Francesco on horseback—great man, founding father—trusting that those of short memory might regard the Sforzas as legitimate rulers. His assignment of Leonardo to the task was thus an important commission. But he paid him little or nothing on account; Leonardo's savings dwindled and he was forced to share commissions with a Milanese artist, Ambrogio da Predis, splitting such fees as came along.

Despite his various rebuffs, Leonardo continued to bombard Lodovico with ideas. From 1484 to 1485 a plague killed about 50,000 of Milan's inhabitants. The reason, Leonardo thought, lay in overcrowding and filth —the streets were heaped with garbage, and sunlight penetrated only briefly into the alleys. He proposed to build a new city, breaking it up into 10 towns of 30,000 each; there would be watercourses to carry off the sewage and the streets would be broad and airy, their width equal to the average height of the houses. (A few centuries later, the County Council of London recognized this as an ideal proportion and ordained it in the laying out of new streets.) Leonardo also proposed a system of high- and low-level roads, the upper for pedestrians and the lower for commercial traffic. He even gave thought to the stairways connecting the levels—they should be spiral, he is said to have remarked, because the vulgar often relieve themselves on landings. If Sforza glanced at Leonardo's highly advanced city plans, no doubt he merely shrugged.

It was in court entertainments that Sforza put Leonardo's talents to great use. This may seem a sad waste of genius to the modern mind, but scenography was well within the painter's domain until the end of the 17th Century, when it became a separate profession. Besides, Leonardo enjoyed it. In 1490 Lodovico married off 20-year-old Gian Galeazzo to Isabella of Aragon, granddaughter of the King of Naples, and for this Leonardo prepared a fantastic display. In one of the halls of the castle he constructed a large mountain with a cleft covered by a curtain. When opened, it revealed a vista of the heavens containing the 12 signs of the zodiac and personifications of the planets; as musicians played, the three Graces and the seven Virtues appeared to praise the bride.

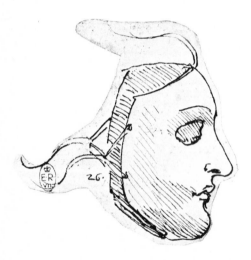

Designed for some long-forgotten festival, this mask is one of many Leonardo undoubtedly made, along with complete costume designs, stage scenery and court decorations, both in Milan and later in France. It has been linked with a cryptic inscription found elsewhere in his notes: "If you value your liberty, do not reveal that my face is the prison of love."

As he gained Sforza's admiration, Leonardo appeared in court not merely as a lutanist and singer but as reciter of satires, jests and "prophecies" which he composed himself. In these he was obliged to work under constraint, tailoring his ideas to fit far duller minds than his own. (Renaissance humor was none too subtle; an example of a great side-splitter, which Leonardo thought funny enough to copy in his journal, concerned an artist who had ugly children but painted beautiful pictures. When asked about the discrepancy, the artist replied he made his pictures by day but his children at night.)

The "prophecies" are actually riddles to which the titles supply the answers. "Many communities there will be who will hide themselves and their young and their victuals within gloomy caverns, and there in dark places will sustain themselves and their families for many months without any light either artificial or natural." After the court had puzzled over this, Leonardo would give the title: "Of Ants."

Some of his prophecies were doubtless never heard. Whatever the morality of the day, it was wise not to offend the Church, and Leonardo had an anticlerical bias. Probably he kept this to himself: "A countless multitude will sell publicly and without hindrance things of the very greatest value, without license from the Lord of these things, which were never theirs nor in their power; and human justice will take no account of this." Title: "Of the Selling of Paradise."

At about this time, when he was engaged in essentially frivolous affairs in the court, there crept into his notes a sense of mortality and the hastening of years. "In rivers, the water that you touch is the last of what has passed," he wrote, "and the first of that which comes: so it is with time present." In another place he asked, "O Leonardo, why so much suffering?" But he was by no means sunk in melancholy. Apparently Sforza began to pay him more, and he found time to follow his intellectual pursuits. He studied an eclipse of the sun, noting that the way to observe one without damage to the eyes is to look through pin-holes in a sheet of paper. In 1490 Sforza sent him to Pavia to give his advice on the construction of the cathedral there; Leonardo remained for six months, engrossed in the great Pavian library, until Sforza summoned him back to Milan to stage another pageant. The occasion was a double wedding— Lodovico, though infatuated with his mistress, Cecilia Gallerani, thought it wise politically to marry the 15-year-old Modenese Beatrice d'Este, Duchess of Bari, and at the same time arranged the wedding of his niece Anna Sforza, to Beatrice's brother Alfonso.

The pageant over, Leonardo pressed on with research that increasingly engrossed him. From his years in Milan date the first of the voluminous notes that together with his art constitute his legacy. He had made some annotated sketches in Florence, but in Milan he began to write down everything that interested him in a random order that presents scholars with an enormous puzzle. He would continue his notebooks to the end of his life, mingling his ideas with those of others, until at last he had what amounted to a loose-leaf encyclopedia with all its pages shuffled. He hoped to put it in order, as a wistful note of 1508 makes plain: "And this [particular book] will be a collection without order, made up of many sheets which I have copied here, hoping afterward to arrange them . . . and I believe that before I am at the end of this, I shall have to repeat the same thing several times; and therefore, O reader, blame me not, because the subjects are many and the memory cannot retain them. . . ."

Leonardo began his *Treatise on Painting* in Milan, reportedly at the request of Sforza, who wanted to know whether sculpture or painting was the nobler art. But Leonardo characteristically did not pursue this project to completion; he may still have been revising the *Treatise* at the time of his death. He constantly interrupted it with other studies, notably mechanics. He devised a machine for making files, a rolling mill to produce sheet iron and a cloth-shearing machine that might have doubled the Duchy's output of fabric. But Lodovico took small interest; instead, he had the great man install a bath in the palace for the wife of Gian Galeazzo.

Sometimes Leonardo dreamed of making fortunes, and committed his ideas to paper with schoolboyish enthusiasm. Industrial mass production was then undreamed of, but he devised a machine for grinding needles at a prodigious rate, using revolving leather belts and an abrasive wheel. "Tomorrow morning on January 2nd, 1496, I will try out the broad belts," he wrote. "A hundred times in each hour, 400 needles make 40,000 per hour, and in 12 hours 480,000. But let us say 400,000, which at five *soldi* for each thousand gives 20,000 *soldi,* that is in total lire 1,000 per day . . . and if one works for 20 days in the month, the yearly total becomes 60,000 ducats"—a great fortune. Nothing came of this.

Leonardo also studied the workings of the human body as well as machinery. He had had some experience of anatomy in Florence, and may have witnessed a dissection. Renaissance artists were concerned with anatomy only as an aid to the representation of the body—pioneers such as Pollaiuolo had worked with cadavers, but had merely flayed them to lay bare the muscular structure, which was all that concerned them. Few men had actually opened the skull, thorax or abdomen. Leonardo's early interest in anatomy went no further than Pollaiuolo's, but the whole thrust of his mind went from the superficial to the intrinsic—once he had learned how something worked, he wished to know why. Thus he approached anatomy with more than an artist's aims.

The procurement of subjects for dissection presented a great problem for him. Modern physicians, analyzing the drawings of his first Milanese period, conclude that the only human material available to him was a head, perhaps from a decapitated criminal, and a leg which may have been severed in combat. The difficulty stemmed from two causes: one was the belief in the literal resurrection of the body and the fear of the awful consequences of dissection; the second lay in the misinterpretation of a bull, *De sepulturis,* issued by Pope Boniface VIII in 1300. The Pope was disturbed by the practice of boiling the bones of crusaders who had died overseas, so that they might more easily be transported home for burial, and he proclaimed excommunication for anyone who engaged in it. Later, the bull was construed as a prohibition of all dissection. The fact is that the Church often tolerated dissection if it was done circumspectly, but was forced to act whenever anyone made an issue of it.

When Leonardo obtained the human head he was still a tyro in anatomy. But he was not content to study only the outside of the skull. In a drawing much admired by practitioners of today, he shows it cut in half, laid open to reveal the placement of the roots of the teeth, the frontal and maxillary sinuses and the nasal cavity—details of no interest to someone who thought of anatomy only as an auxiliary to painting.

Mathematics occupied much of his time in his last years with Sforza. His closest associate, it is said, was a Franciscan named Luca Pacioli, a friend of artists and a professor of mathematics. During their relationship Pacioli wrote a textbook, *On Divine Proportion,* for which Leonardo drew the illustrations; they consisted mainly of polyhedrons, which were thought to have a supernatural significance beyond geometry. In mathematics Leonardo sought the proof of all his theories. "There is no certainty where one can neither apply any of the mathematical sciences nor any of those which are based upon mathematical sciences," he wrote. He was wary of generalities, preferring to adduce a half-dozen proofs of a fact or situation to the making of any flat statement, and he scorned the involuted disputation that so often preoccupied Renaissance thinkers. "He who blames the supreme certainty of mathematics feeds on confusion," he wrote, "and will never impose silence on the contradictions of the sophistical sciences, which occasion a perpetual clamor."

In Milan Leonardo moved from place to place, sometimes living in Sforza's castle. He had apprentices and servants, his household at one time numbering at least six. Among these was a 10-year-old boy named Gian Giacomo de' Caprotti, who came to live with him as an apprentice painter in 1490, when Leonardo was 38. "This was a graceful and beautiful youth," wrote Vasari, "with fine, curly hair, in which Leonardo greatly

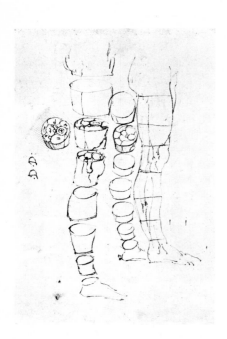

Leonardo's cross-sectional rendering of a man's right leg is the first known example of a technique still widely used for the study of anatomy. Although Leonardo numbered various parts of one segment of the leg for reference, his notes identifying them have not been found.

delighted." But the youth's behavior did not match his appearance. Leonardo nicknamed him "Salai"—little Satan—and referred to him as "thievish, lying, obstinate, greedy." Soon after Salai's arrival Leonardo had some clothes made for the boy, who came from a poor family: "I had two shirts cut out for him, a pair of hose and a doublet, and when I put money aside to pay for these things he stole the money. . . . He stole a style worth 22 *soldi*. . . . It was of silver." During Salai's first year with him, Leonardo bought him a cloak, six shirts, three doublets and no fewer than 24 pairs of shoes, but Salai continued to steal whatever he could lay his hands on.

The relationship between Leonardo and Salai lasted for almost 25 years. Leonardo ceaselessly catered to him, lending or giving him money. The youth had no talent, and if he occasionally produced a second-rate work, Leonardo indulgently touched it up. In the endless series of paired profiles that Leonardo drew, the face of the old man became increasingly grim and that of the pretty youth became Salai.

As his years with Sforza drew to a close Leonardo was beset by financial troubles. Lodovico was embroiled in numerous costly deals to maintain power and could—or would—no longer pay his artists. Leonardo wrote him beseeching letters; one (torn vertically with one part lost, so that we have only the first half of each line) reveals his sad position: "My Lord, knowing the mind of Your Excellency to be occupied . . . to remind Your Lordship of my small matters, and I should have maintained silence . . . my life to your service I hold myself ever ready to obey. . . . Of the horse I will say nothing because I know the times . . . to Your Lordship how my salary is now two years in arrear of . . . works of fame by which I could show to those who are to come that I have been. . . ." Lodovico could feign lack of understanding; he did so.

The polyhedron, one of the most intriguing of three-dimensional geometric figures, appears in many forms in Leonardo's illustrations for Fra Luca Pacioli's book *On Divine Proportion*. To him, proportions were of basic importance "not only . . . in numbers and measurements but also in sounds, weights, positions and in whatsoever power there may be."

Sforza's usurped dukedom was slipping away from him because of miscalculations that shrewder men—Lorenzo de' Medici, for example—would never have made. The Kingdom of Naples was in arms against him, and he had offended the papacy and Florence as well. In foolish desperation, Sforza in 1494 bribed the King of France, Charles VIII, who had an ancestral claim to the throne of Naples, to come to his aid. Charles was willing, but as he marched through Lombardy on his way to Naples he noted the wealth of Milan, and not surprisingly remembered that France had an old claim to that state too. Charles did not live to make it good, although he did seize and briefly hold Naples. In a panic, realizing the dreadful blunder he had made in inviting the avaricious French into Italy, Sforza joined with his former enemies and drove Charles back beyond the Alps. But the blunder was fatal. In 1499 Charles's successor, Louis XII, descended on Milan and Sforza was done. He was taken off to France a prisoner; tradition has it that he spent his last days carving the words *Infelix Sum* (I am wretched) on the stone wall of a jail.

Leonardo remained briefly in Milan and made a few impersonal notes on the wreckage, ending with a reference to his former patron: "The Duke has lost his state and his possessions and his liberty, and has seen none of his works finished." Then, with Luca Pacioli—and Salai—he returned to Florence, going by way of Mantua and Venice to see the sights.

Il Moro's Magician

Lodovico Sforza once remarked that the Pope was his chaplain, the Holy Roman Emperor his general, and the King of France his errand boy. Of this colossal vanity, his castle was the symbol: huge and grim, it was the center of Milanese life. Behind its walls, as in some massive strongbox, there gleamed treasures to delight the mind and eye. Beautiful women and curious dwarfs, diamonds and astrologers, paintings, poets and emeralds all combined to make the court one of the most glittering in Italy—indeed, in all Europe.

The greatest treasure of his court, although the Duke was not aware of it, was Leonardo da Vinci. In Leonardo, Sforza had at his command a magician who could conjure up whatever was desired—pageant or picture, music or mechanism. To be sure, this was a highly independent and erratic magician; one might ask him for a statue of a man on horseback, and find him instead painting a portrait of a musician or devising some unheard-of weapon. Patrons could not manage Leonardo. Sforza was no more successful than any other.

A glimpse of the Duke, his wife Beatrice d'Este and their son Massimiliano, together with an anonymous artist's conception of Milanese courtly life, appears on the next two pages. Following that may be seen a sampling of Leonardo's work of the period—creations strange and beautiful, which have long outlived the pomp and vainglory of Lodovico Sforza.

On a tower of Sforza's castle is the emblem of the Visconti, the previous rulers of Milan. When Lodovico's father, the *condottiere* Francesco Sforza, took power, he added the viper to his arms. As a reminder of strength and guile it suited the Sforzas as well as the Visconti; it shows a serpent with a Saracen in its jaws.

Beatrice meanwhile hurled herself like a meteor into the life of the Milanese court, delighting in masquerades, pageants and balls. The girl loved sports and hunting, avidly collected rare silverwork, glass and musical instruments, and had a vast wardrobe of dresses embroidered with gold and jewels. After two years of marriage she bore Lodovico a son, his first legitimate child and heir; *Il Moro* was so overjoyed that he caused all the bells of Milan to ring for six days. But motherhood did nothing to slow the hectic pace of Beatrice's life. Her wild whirl of amusements continued at an even faster pace, perhaps because the inconstant Lodovico had taken yet another mistress, Lucrezia Crivelli. In 1497 Beatrice suddenly became ill at a ball, retired to her chamber, gave birth to a stillborn child and died at 22.

Master of the Pala Sforzesca: Portrait of Beatrice d'Este, detail from the *Sforza Altarpiece*, c. 1495

The Horse, Leonardo's gigantic piece of sculpture for Lodovico Sforza, kept him intermittently at work for almost 16 years. Although not a trace remains of the nearly 26-foot-high clay model he made, many of his studies for *Il Cavallo* still exist, including these drawings now in the possession of the British Crown. Both of those shown here are in silverpoint, an extremely exacting medium which Leonardo handled with a grace and freshness particularly evident in the study for a rearing horse below. Prancing or rearing horses had an enduring fascination for him; dozens of them, some mere doodles and others elaborately worked, are scattered through the sketch sheets he made from youth to old age. However, when he began to think of them in sculptural rather than in graphic terms, he was obliged to deal with problems of weight and balance. He suggests below that the horse's forelegs may be supported by a fallen warrior, and in other drawings he experimented with tree stumps. Later he abandoned the prancing design and turned to the traditional walking or standing horse, painstakingly studied in profile and front view on the sheet reproduced on the opposite page.

A horseman trampling on a fallen foe; study for *The Horse*, c. 1490

A horse and its forelegs; study for *The Horse*, c. 1488

In decorating the vaulted ceiling of the *Sala delle Asse* in Sforza's castle, Leonardo created an eye-whirling bower of intertwining boughs. The frescoed canopy covers 2,880 square feet and includes coats of arms and decorative

inscriptions. At a casual glance it appears that there are several separate knots of golden rope in the design, but in fact the rope is unbroken, turning, doubling back and writhing throughout the whole fantastic pattern.

Portrait of a Musician, c. 1485

Youth with a lance, c. 1513

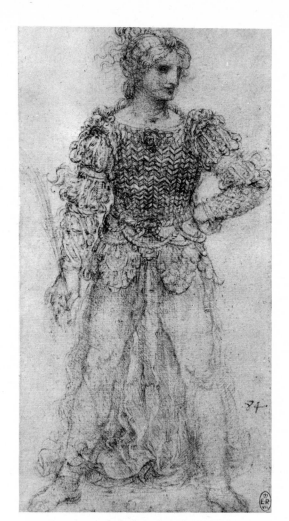

Figure wearing a bodice of interlaced ribbons, c. 1513

During his early years in Milan Leonardo painted the *Portrait of a Musician* on the opposite page. The name of the young man is unknown, and there is no record that anyone commissioned the work. However, the face is quite similar to that of the angel in the *Madonna of the Rocks (pages 50-51)*, and it may be that Leonardo, by chance encountering an individual who embodied his ideal of beauty, simply seized the chance to paint him. There is great subtlety in the modeling of the face and in the use of light falling on its planes. Evidently it was the face alone that interested the artist; the rest of the portrait is unfinished.

In the field of court art Leonardo was later repeatedly engaged in designing and producing pageants, masques and allegorical tableaux. The drawings on this page are costume studies for such affairs, but their meaning and contexts can no longer be fathomed. The style and medium of the drawings —the two at right are in black chalk, while that above combines black chalk, wash and ink on an oatmeal-colored paper—indicate that they were made around 1512 or later, long after Sforza's downfall. At that time Leonardo was in the service of the French, and it is thought that he may have redrawn and improved the designs that once delighted *Il Moro* in order to present them to his late patron's conquerors.

Man with a club and shackled feet, c. 1511

Knot, engraving after Leonardo, c. 1499

These drawings epitomize Leonardo's lifelong interest in the intricate and the allegorical. The prodigiously complex ornament above—except for the elements in the center and each corner—is actually composed of only four continuous lines. The meaning of the inscription is unclear; it suggests that he conducted an academy, of which this might have been the seal. However, history has no record of it. The design is typically Leonardesque, but may also have been executed by one of his pupils.

On the opposite page appears one of the many cryptic

Implements rained down on the earth from the clouds, c. 1498

but certainly accusatory drawings he made concerning the materialism of mankind. At the top, in his mirror writing, appear the words, "On this side Adam and on that Eve." Some critics profess to see two roughly drawn human figures in the tumultuous sky; others are content to admit that they see nothing at all. From this ambiguous sky falls a rain of implements, including rakes, musical instruments, pincers and spectacles. On the ground below Leonardo has written: "Oh human misery; of how many things you make yourself the slave for money!"

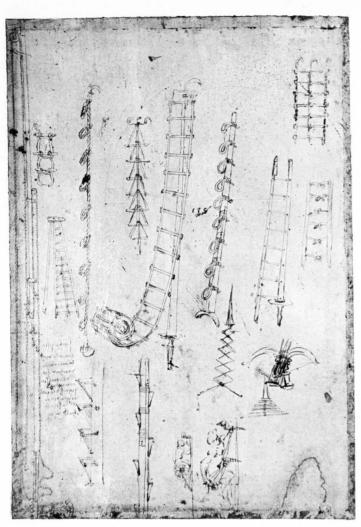

Rope ladders and pinions for scaling a wall, c. 1478

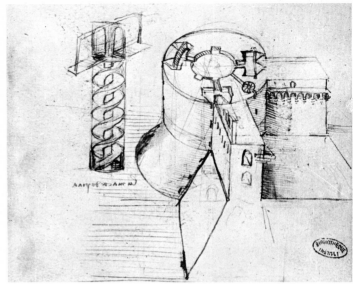

Detail of a corner tower of a fortress, c. 1488

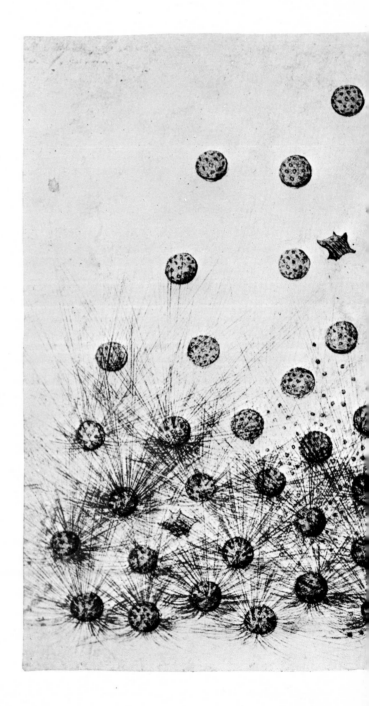

Although Lodovico Sforza seems not to have accepted any of them, Leonardo offered him an astonishing quantity and range of military ideas. Some, like the array of scaling ladders above, were merely improvements on equipment already commonly employed. The tank at the top of the opposite page, with its armor and breech-loading guns, was hundreds of years ahead of its time in concept, but its hand-turned cranks, shown in a sketch of the vehicle upside down, could scarcely have provided adequate power or speed.

However, Leonardo's designs for conical missiles with fins and the explosive mortar bombs, at right, were quite practical, as posterity to its sorrow would eventually discover. Among Renaissance weaponeers Leonardo may well have been alone in his grasp of the fact that increasingly powerful and accurate big guns would soon make the old-fashioned, high-walled castle obsolete. His sketch of a fortress tower on this page, with its low and unusually thick walls, curved and slanted to deflect shot, clearly showed what was to come. The tower is so obviously designed to contain circular stairs that one may at first wonder why he troubled to make a separate sketch of them, but a close look reveals his intent and his genius: the spiral is double so that the soldiers ascending and descending would not collide with each other.

Covered armored car, c. 1485

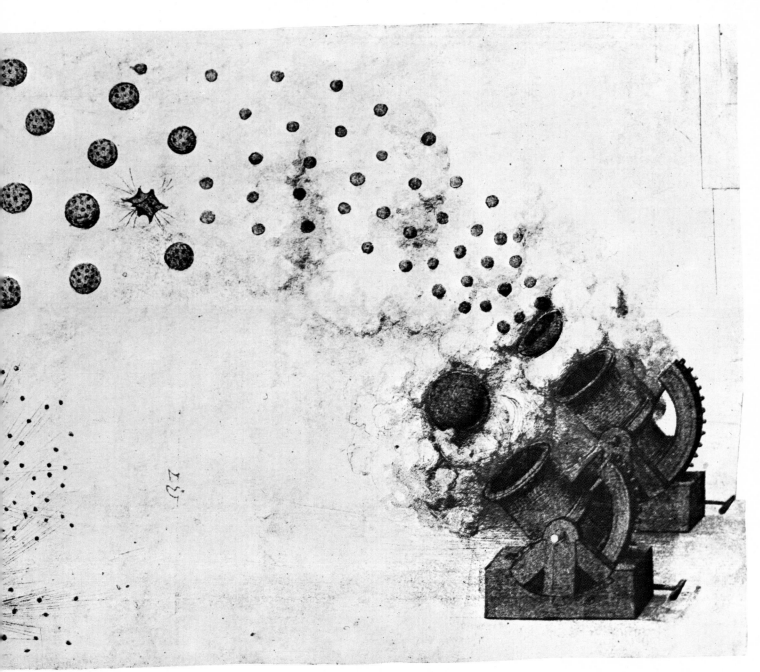

Mortars with explosive projectiles, c. 1490

Milan, refectory of Santa Maria delle Grazie, after bombing of August 14, 1943

Milan, refectory of Santa Maria delle Grazie, after restoration

IV

Grandeur
and Tragedy

In 1943 an air raid reduced the
monastery of Santa Maria delle
Grazie to rubble; miraculously, the
Last Supper, protected by sandbags on
the rear wall *(left, above)*, survived.
Today, with the monastery restored,
the painting may once again be seen
in its original setting. The filled-in
doorway at the bottom of the picture
was cut in the 17th Century when
the *Last Supper* had so disintegrated
that the monks no longer considered
it worth saving.

It may seem that Leonardo's 17 years under Sforza were frustrating and
unprofitable if one considers only the machines that were never built,
the ideas not adopted and the ephemera of his court art. But it was during this period that he produced the *Last Supper*, for which the lifelong
labor of a thousand ordinary men would be a trifling price. The painting
was made rapidly (for Leonardo) in the final years before he left Milan;
his artistic genius, however, did not lie fallow until that time. The Louvre
version of the *Madonna of the Rocks* was apparently done early in his
stay in the city, and in 1483, when he had been there about a year, he
commenced work on Sforza's dream, *The Horse*—which from an entirely different viewpoint was Leonardo's dream as well.

There existed in northern Italy a Gothic tradition of aristocratic tombs
surmounted by equestrian figures, one of which, that of Bernabò Visconti,
survives in Milan today. It may well be that Lodovico had it in mind to
place his father in this knightly tradition. But artistically, in the form of
freestanding monuments to the glory of individuals, there were but few
equestrian statues that might be considered precursors of Leonardo's work.
Of these, one was a classical antique in Rome. Having survived the depre-
dations of waves of conquering barbarians and the religious zeal of early
medieval Christians who mutilated sculptures (usually by knocking off
their noses) in the belief that they were idols, the mounted figure of *Marcus Aurelius* stood as an example and a challenge to sculptors of Leonardo's
day. (The *Marcus Aurelius* was not damaged because Christians mistakenly thought it a statue of Constantine, the first Roman Emperor of their
own faith.) Although he had doubtless read descriptions and perhaps seen
sketches of it, Leonardo had not yet seen the actual bronze.

There were two other statues that may also have served Leonardo as
guides. In Padua was Donatello's monument to *Gattamelata,* a famous
mercenary general—but of this, too, Leonardo had only secondhand
knowledge. In Venice stood the *Colleoni (page 39),* a tribute to another
general, the only one of the three equestrian statues Leonardo knew well.
Even in this case he had not studied the completed work, but it was a
commission that had come into Verrocchio's shop while Leonardo was still

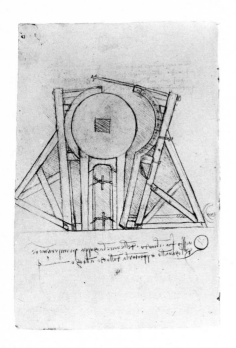

Many scholars have doubted that Leonardo ever had sufficiently detailed plans to be able to carry out his scheme to cast the colossal Sforza horse statue. But in March 1967, 700 long-lost pages from his notebooks were re-discovered in Madrid's National Library. Among them were the sketches shown here and on the opposite page. Above is Leonardo's drawing for the bracing of the heavy mold for the horse's body, seen in cross-section. Below is his apparatus for lowering the mold to its side, preparatory to pouring the molten bronze.

in Florence; he had seen the drawings and models for it, and perhaps even made suggestions.

The earlier statues are quite different in spirit but have two things in common—they are approximately life-sized *(Marcus Aurelius* is a bit larger), and, in each, one of the forelegs of the horse is raised. Originally, according to tradition, under the foreleg of the Roman horse lay the body of a prostrate enemy. In Donatello's work the foreleg rests on a ball. In Verrocchio's, latest of the three, there is no support at all—a commonplace design today, but scarcely so in the Early Renaissance, when an incomplete knowledge of statics obliged sculptors to be very careful with the equilibrium of their statues.

Although he shared some of the technical limitations of his predecessors, Leonardo determined to surpass them in a way that would astonish the world. His equestrian statue was not merely to be an object of incredible beauty; it was to be the largest and most daring ever conceived. In scale it was to have been Homeric—more than twice that of the earlier monuments. And in these colossal dimensions Leonardo planned to place the horse not in a walking or pacing position, but in the act of rearing with both forelegs off the ground.

In preparation for this unheard-of feat, Leonardo studied long and carefully the fine horses in the stables of Sforza's noblemen, meanwhile producing a handsomely illustrated treatise on equine anatomy. He also devoted much time to the problem of balance, sketching the rider seated well back on the horse with his arm, holding a weapon, extended to the rear in an effort to shift the center of gravity. At times he seems to have despaired of solving the static problem and drew a crouching, supporting figure beneath the horse's forelegs. But always the rider was active, standing or whirling about in the saddle as though commanding men in the pitch of battle. Contemporaries who were aware of his work believed the statue could never be cast—a few years later Michelangelo, encountering Leonardo in Florence, taunted him with, "You made a design for a horse to be cast in bronze, and, unable to cast it, you have in your shame abandoned it. And to think that those Milanese capons believed you!"

Indeed it never was cast, but there is good evidence that Leonardo could have accomplished the casting. One problem would have been to get an estimated 200,000 pounds of molten metal into the mold fast enough and at such a high temperature that it would not cool irregularly and botch the work: he tackled this by designing a system of multiple furnaces. In a fragmentary treatise called "Of Weight" he worked out the problem of equilibrium; his sketches show iron braces within the hollow statue, and his knowledge of gravity was sufficient for the task.

Finally, however, Leonardo abandoned the idea of a rearing horse and reverted to a walking one for other reasons. The statue was intended, after all, to be a piece of visual propaganda that would make heroic the memory of Lodovico's father. Had the horse been rearing, might not all eyes have been fixed on that fantastic creation, to the disadvantage of the rider? More than a century after Leonardo's death the idea was risked in Spain, where the first equestrian monument with a rearing horse was erected around 1640 by Pietro Tacca in honor of King Philip IV. The static problem was solved by the scientist Galileo, who used computations very similar to Leonardo's and gave them to Tacca. It was not until 1782, however, that something approaching Leonardo's conception was achieved, in Etienne-Maurice Falconet's monument to Peter the Great in St. Petersburg. Tacca's earlier statue, although the first of its kind, had been immobile and reserved in pose; Falconet's is full of a dash and spirit that would have pleased Leonardo. But to this day, nothing of the scale and quality he envisioned has been created.

By November 1493, Leonardo had completed a full-sized model of the walking horse, without its rider, which was exhibited at the marriage festivities of one of the Sforzas. The impact was enormous and ironic; in no time Leonardo became famous, and soon his reputation spread throughout Italy. The *Adoration of the Magi* and the Louvre *Madonna of the Rocks* had not gained him much credit, but now a model of a horse, no doubt exquisitely executed and certainly very large, but still a model of a horse, finally won him at 41 the recognition he had long sought. Of the power and beauty of his creation only hints remain in the drawings he made *(pages 64-65)*; masterfully exact, yet enormously expressive and romantically fired, they are among the finest any artist has produced.

The history of the huge model is short and sad. Lodovico Sforza had been collecting the vast weight of bronze required for its casting, but in 1494 he was obliged to send it all to his brother-in-law, Ercole d'Este, to be made into cannon. For a few more years the model remained intact in Milan, one of the marvels of the Italian world. But in 1499 when the French overwhelmed the city, a troop of ignorant Gascon bowmen discovered it, and, drunk with victory and Lombard wine, they used it as a target. Their arrows pocked the statue with innumerable holes through which water might enter; after a few seasons of warm rain and bitter freeze the great horse fell apart and became nothing but a shapeless mound.

Leonardo's work on the horse was continually interrupted, partly because of his constitutional inability to keep his attention focused on so lengthy a project and in part because of other demands Sforza made on his talent. He appears to have served for a time as official court portraitist; the first of his works in that capacity was a painting of Lodovico's mistress Cecilia Gallerani, probably painted in 1484.

Cecilia was then only about 17, but had already been seduced by Lodovico, had borne him a son and occupied a commanding position in his court. The portrait, known as the *Lady with an Ermine (page 52)*, strongly suggests the qualities Cecilia was reported to have had: her face is keenly attentive and intelligent, her fingers long and sensuous, those of a musician and a voluptuary. The background has been repainted, possibly by the none-too-skilled Milanese artist Ambrogio da Predis with whom Leonardo collaborated; the result is that the face is sharply outlined in black with none of the misty effects and chiaroscuro of Leonardo. However, the modeling of the face and particularly of the ermine reveals the work as unquestionably his. The pivotal turning of the lady's head against her shoulders and torso and, above all, the serpentine pose of the animal could only have been invented by Leonardo. The size of the ermine and

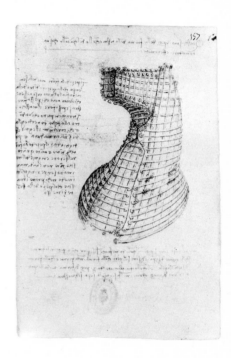

Because of the immense size of the Sforza horse—finished it would have stood nearly 26 feet high—Leonardo planned to cast it in pieces. His sketch above shows an intricate framework of iron strips that he designed to reinforce the plaster mold for the head and neck section. Among the newly recovered pages is Leonardo's note, dated December 20, 1493, that he was ready to undertake the casting. Regrettably, his patron had other needs for the bronze; the horse was never completed.

the proximity of its sharp, vicious snout to the lady's throat are somewhat alarming; perhaps Leonardo intended to suggest the precarious status of court favorites (himself included); perhaps, too, he saw a parallel between the characters of woman and weasel—their cool eyes and pointed faces are bent in the same direction. There is no doubt, however, as to why he put the animal into the painting. The ermine is described in old bestiaries as being of such a pure nature that it will suffer capture or death rather than crawl into a muddy hole. Sforza, with a stunted sense of irony, adopted the ermine as his symbol.

In the weaselish course of events Cecilia Gallerani was replaced in Sforza's affection first by a wife and then by another mistress, Lucrezia Crivelli, whose portrait Leonardo also painted. The whereabouts of this work is much debated today; several critics believe it is a portrait in the Louvre, long mislabeled *La Belle Ferronnière* because of an old error that identified the lady not as a mistress of Sforza but of Francis I of France. It is not an example of Leonardo at his best—Bernard Berenson remarked that "one would regret to have to accept this as Leonardo's own work." But, as Leonardo sometimes was obliged to do, he may here have sacrificed his genius to the fashion of Milanese courtly portraiture, which dictated a stiff, unlifelike pose and set great store on showiness of dress and jewels. He painted these perfunctorily except where he found a detail that interested him, such as the curling ribbons on the lady's shoulder. The painting was much admired and widely copied in the 19th Century, but none of the copyists succeeded in duplicating the lovely modeling of the face.

There remains one more portrait from Leonardo's early Milanese years, perhaps the least important of all his paintings and lacking in documentation, but as fate has arranged it, the best preserved: the *Portrait of a Musician* in Milan's Ambrosiana *(page 68)*. Only the face is finished; it is of the type of Leonardo's angels, although a good deal more masculine, and its luminous shadows suggest what might be seen today in his major works if overpainting and varnish had not obscured them. Some years ago when the painting was cleaned, several notes of music materialized on the paper the man holds in his hand; Leonardo scholars of the microscopic school, knowing his fondness for puzzles and secret things, have tried vainly to read a message into them.

Puzzles, or rather an incredibly intricate series of interwoven designs, are the feature of an anomalous piece of work Leonardo produced in one of the great rooms of Sforza's castle, the *Sala delle Asse*. It is not a painting in the ordinary sense, but it so far transcends interior decoration that there is no adequate phrase for it *(pages 66-67)*.

For the walls and vaulting of the *Sala delle Asse* Leonardo designed (much of the work was probably executed by his pupils) a green bower of willow trees; their branches and tendrils fantastically intertwine, and among them are delicate ropes twisting in endless knots and loops. The effect is almost aural, like a musical fugue. Possibly Leonardo, who spent days and perhaps weeks drawing similar puzzle-patterns on paper, intended them as a sort of personal signet: one meaning of *vinci* is "willow," and hence wickerwork. His designs in Sforza's hall appear to have

This Leonardo drawing of an ermine and a hunter illustrates a popular allegory and one which Lodovico, Duke of Milan, used as reference to himself; the ermine was one of his heraldic devices. In the tale, the ermine, symbolizing purity, suffers itself to be beaten and captured rather than become dirty by escaping from the hunter through the mud.

no other hidden significance. In time the paint faded and flaked away—the hall was long used as a barracks—but enough of the designs remained so that they could be restored in 1901, and further restoration was in progress in 1965. The new painting does not quite convey the sense of writhing, organic life that Leonardo must originally have achieved, but it remains a fascinating subject to study.

Architecture occupied much of Leonardo's attention in Milan. As architect and engineer for Sforza, he supervised the completion and renovation of buildings and gave his advice about fortifications. Even when he was engrossed in studies for the *Last Supper* his thoughts were divided between painting and architecture, as some sketches for that work show.

In 1488, along with Bramante and others, he presented plans and a wooden model (which he later withdrew) in the competition for the design of the central cupola of the Milan cathedral. At that time he was a friend of Bramante, who like himself was an imported artist, and who later became the foremost architect of the High Renaissance. In the association between them it is difficult to tell who influenced the other, but it would seem that the stronger of the two was Bramante. None of Leonardo's building designs was ever executed, whereas Bramante has several to his credit, ranging from the exquisite little domed Tempietto in Rome to the colossal St. Peter's (for which his plans, after his death, were modified by Michelangelo and others).

Bramante and Leonardo, like other Early Renaissance architects before them, were preoccupied with uniting the square and the circle (dome), the two "perfect" geometrical forms. The slow working-out of this problem can be seen in Leonardo's Milanese sketches, which have great historic importance, for they alone trace the transition from the Early to the High Renaissance in architecture. Leonardo's *Project for a Church,* a pen drawing in the Bibliothèque de l'Arsenal in Paris, stands midway between the plan of Brunelleschi for the dome of the Florence cathedral and the Bramante-Michelangelo design for St. Peter's.

In his other church designs Leonardo developed his taste for radiating circular motifs to a logical extreme—some of his sketches are so full of domes that they suggest the clustered cupolas of Byzantine and Russian church architecture.

In nonchurch architecture, Leonardo's fastidious nature, although not his interest in the activity itself, led him to design the most secular of buildings: a bawdyhouse. His constant wanderings in search of beautiful, grotesque or corrupt faces evidently led him into Milan's red-light district, where he observed that the customary, haphazard plans of bordellos left much to be desired. In consequence, he designed a house with right-angled corridors and three separate entrances, so that the clientele could come and go with smaller risk of embarrassing meetings.

A final architectural whim of Leonardo's was a mausoleum for princes on an Egyptian scale. (He had a strange fixation on the East; he wrote letters and tales which seem deliberately intended to give the reader the false impression that he had traveled there, and at one time he seriously proposed to the Sultan of Turkey that he build a titanic bridge across the Bosporus, so high that tall-masted ships could sail under it and fearful men refuse to walk on it.) His mausoleum was conical in shape, about 2,000 feet in diameter at its base and 500 feet high, surmounted by a circular temple and colonnade. Whatever led him to conceive this is unknown; there are a few notes and a drawing, and then the idea vanishes.

In 1495, at the request of Lodovico Sforza, Leonardo began the *Last Supper (pages 85-93)* on the wall of the refectory in the Dominican monastery of Santa Maria delle Grazie in Milan. The painting is so prodigious both in fact and in its influence, so familiar throughout the Western world, that discussing it is like saying a few words about the Atlantic Ocean. Nonetheless one might begin by pointing out a fact so obvious that it is often overlooked: in all art there are few, if any, compositional problems more difficult than the presenting of 13 men seated at a straight table. In Leonardo's hands the problem is so beautifully solved that it does not appear to exist; an amateur of art, if he can possibly erase the memory of the *Last Supper* from his mind, might attempt an independent solution to see precisely how formidable that problem is.

A second difficulty is to make the isolation of Judas apparent at a glance. For perhaps a thousand years before Leonardo, from the very beginnings of Christian art, this requirement had generally been met by placing Christ and the 11 faithful disciples on one side of the table and Judas on the other. Even the artists of the Early Renaissance, who broke away from the traditional rendering of religious themes, could as a rule find no better solution—it is still seen in what are perhaps the best of the Quattrocento *Last Suppers,* those of Andrea del Castagno and of Domenico Ghirlandaio, Michelangelo's teacher. Castagno *(page 96),* in his oppressive and cramping background, moved toward a new idea. He painted a series of six marble panels above the heads of the figures; five are of ordinary pattern, but the one above Christ and Judas is wildly mottled like the sky during a thunderstorm. Nonetheless Judas still sits alone on the opposite side of the table.

Leonardo had been developing his ideas for his *Last Supper* for some 15 years; in one of his sketches for the *Adoration of the Magi* there appears a group of servants in animated discussion at a table, and nearby is a figure of Christ. As he came closer to the moment of facing the blank wall in Santa Maria delle Grazie he must have made many preliminary sketches; of these, a number of studies for individual heads survive, but only two for the entire composition. The latter reveal that almost until he began to paint he was still thinking of isolating Judas physically; but then his genius intervened.

Leonardo had also devoted an incalculable amount of thought to the revelation of human emotions in painting. One of the key sentences in his *Treatise* is this: "The painter has two objectives, man and the intention of his soul. The first is easy, the latter hard, because he has to represent it by the movements of the limbs." Mere grimaces were of no interest to him except in his sketches of grotesques; in motion, gesture, could be found the means to express feeling. This is a singularly Italian concept, as the great German poet Goethe notes in his essay on the *Last Supper.* "In [Leonardo's] nation, the whole body is animated, every member, every limb participates in any expression of feeling, of passion, and even of thought. By a varied position and motion of the hands, the Italian signifies: *What do I care!—Come!—This is a rogue—take care of him!—His life shall not be long!—This is the point!—Attend to this, ye that hear me!*

"Such a national peculiarity could not but attract the notice of Leonardo, who was in the highest degree alive to everything that appeared characteristic, and in this particular, the picture before us is strikingly distinguished, so that it is impossible, with this view, sufficiently to contemplate it."

In his notes for the painting Leonardo enumerated several gestures he thought suitable—some he retained, others were dropped. "One who was drinking has left his glass in its position and turned his head toward the speaker [eliminated]. Another twists the fingers of his hands together and turns with a frown to his companion [eliminated]. Another with hands spread open showing the palm, shrugs his shoulders up to his ears and makes a mouth of astonishment [St. Andrew]. Another speaks into his neighbor's ear and the listener turns to him to lend an ear, while he holds a knife in one hand [St. Peter] . . . and in turning round, another, who holds a knife, upsets with his hand a glass on the table." The last gesture was retained, but changed and assigned to Judas, who clutches not a knife but a moneybag and instead of a glass upsets the salt, in the traditional, superstitious symbolism of impending evil.

The faces in the painting, with the exception of Christ's, are reportedly those of actual people Leonardo sought out in and near Milan. For the Lord he apparently considered two men: "Christ: Count Giovanni, who belongs to the household of the Cardinal of Mortaro. . . . Alessandro Carissimo of Parma for the hand of Christ." In the end, Christ appeared as an abstract; a deeply moving, universally appealing figure that Leonardo somehow summoned up through the mantle of cool withdrawal that appeared to enclose Him. To locate an appropriate Judas, Leonardo spent so much time wandering through the haunts of Milanese criminals that the prior of Santa Maria delle Grazie complained to Sforza of his "laziness." To this Leonardo replied that he was indeed having difficulty finding a Judas, but if pressed, he could use the head of the prior, which would do very nicely.

An accusation of dilatoriness, at least in the case of the *Last Supper,* could only have been made by a man who knew nothing of the workings of genius. Leonardo completed the great painting in three years or perhaps less, during which the project was constantly in his mind. The Italian writer Matteo Bandello, who attended the priory school as a boy and watched Leonardo at work, described him thus: "He would often come to the convent at early dawn. . . . Hastily mounting the scaffolding, he worked diligently till the shades of evening compelled him to cease, never thinking of food at all, so absorbed was he in his work. At other times he would remain there three or four days without touching his picture, only coming for a few hours to remain before it, with folded arms, gazing at his figures as if to criticize himself. At midday, too, when the glare of the sun at its zenith had made bare all the streets of Milan, I have seen him hasten from the castle, where he was modeling his

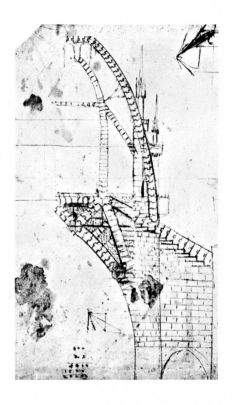

Leonardo the architect here worked out a problem for the construction of the dome of the Milan cathedral. This cross section was probably made in connection with Leonardo's entry in a competition to select an architect; he withdrew before the judging, for reasons unknown.

colossal horse, without seeking the shade, by the shortest way to the convent, where he would add a touch or two and immediately return."

In addition to using living models for the disciples, Leonardo surrounded them with objects then in everyday use, dispensing with all archaic imaginings. The wall on which he painted was in the dining hall of the convent; the *Last Supper* occupied one narrow end of the rectangular refectory and at the other, facing it, stood the table of the prior on a raised dais. Between them, running the length of the room, were the tables of the monks. In the painting the tablecloth, knives, forks, glassware and china were all similar to those of the monks themselves. It was Leonardo's conception that there, in that company, Christ the Spiritual Prior would eat the food of mortal men. The effect of the painting, at least as it appeared at the time of its completion in 1498, must have been an overwhelming reversal of reality and illusion: the actual room became an extension of the picture.

Of the two problems that for centuries had confronted painters of Last Suppers, the isolation of Judas was the one more easily solved by Leonardo. He placed Judas on the same side of the table as all the other figures, but cut him off in a psychological aloneness that is far more devastating than mere physical separation could ever be. Dark, staring, he leans away from Christ, forever sealed in his guilt and solitude. The other disciples, questioning, remonstrating, denying, have as yet no knowledge of who the betrayer is; the spectator sees at once.

The arrangement of the figures, which are half again as large as life, has much of Leonardo's mathematics in it. At the center, Christ, with arms stretched out and down, is a triangle; the central vanishing point is behind His head, above which the light from the main window and its arched pediment form the equivalent of a halo. The 12 disciples are divided into two groups of six; with Christ, they make a combination of three units. But the groups of disciples are subdivided; they fall into four internal compositions, again of three units each.

The traditional interpretation of the painting is that Christ has just spoken the words, "One of you shall betray me," and that Leonardo chose to fix that exact moment for all time. The disciples react to the words with a magnificent display of pose and gesture, revealing "the intention of their souls"—or, as the phrase is sometimes unfelicitously translated, "the state of their minds."

Beyond the freezing of one dramatic moment, Leonardo apparently had other, deeper meanings in mind. One of these is Christ's central act at the Last Supper, the institution of Holy Communion—"And as they were eating, Jesus took bread . . . and gave it to the disciples and said, Take and eat; this is my body. And He took the cup . . . saying, Drink ye all of it; for this is my blood. . . ." His gesture is one of offering, and of submission to the Divine will that made necessary His betrayal and crucifixion. The mathematician Luca Pacioli, Leonardo's friend who watched the execution of the painting, wrote of it as "a symbol of man's burning desire for salvation."

There is a final, technical aspect of the painting that testifies to Leonardo's genius—if that were necessary. The area with which he had to deal was a difficult one, approximately 14 by 30 feet, requiring very skillful handling of the background architecture. Andrea del Castagno, faced with more or less the same shape, appears to have conceived his background first and then crammed the figures into it, with the result that they sit in a monotonous row like men in a subway car. Leonardo drew his figures first and then provided a background that, for all its limitations in true height on the wall, seems spacious and almost airy—a masterpiece of linear perspective.

As it originally appeared, the *Last Supper* must have been incomparably beautiful—Leonardo worked not in fresco but in tempera, employing all the rich color effects the technique allows. But in order to paint on the stone wall he found it necessary first to cover the wall with some material that would hold the medium and protect the painting from moisture. To this end he compounded an experimental mixture of pitch and mastic—and that was the beginning of one of the greatest tragedies in the history of art. Santa Maria delle Grazie had been hastily rebuilt on Sforza's order; the masons had filled the walls with moisture-retaining rubble, full of the acids and salts that exude from lime and old bricks. Also, the monastery stands on low ground—Goethe noted that in 1800 after a heavy rainstorm water stood two feet deep in the room containing the *Last Supper,* and surmised that the chronicled great deluge of 1500 that occurred soon after the completion of the painting caused similar if not worse flooding. Inexorably the moisture and the corrosive exudations did their work; the paint began to flake away from the wall. In 1556, when Vasari observed it, he noted that "there is nothing visible except a muddle of blots." A century later it was written that one could scarcely distinguish the subject, let alone the details, of the painting.

During the 17th and 18th Centuries the *Last Supper* was restored many times by inept artists. Sir Kenneth Clark points out a few of the gloomy consequences: "In the painting [as it appears at present] St. Peter, with his villainously low forehead, is one of the most disturbing figures in the whole composition; but the [early] copies show that his head was originally tilted back in foreshortening. The restorer was unable to follow this difficult piece of drawing and has rendered it as a deformity." In the case of St. Andrew, the original profile has been turned into a three-quarter view—the repainter has "made the dignified old man into an appalling type of simian hypocrisy." The head of St. James the Less is not Leonardo's creation at all, but the work of an unknown hand.

The outlines of the mighty figures still remain. Between 1946 and 1954 they were again restored by Mauro Pellicioli, a master of the art, and what may now be seen, as through a glass clouded with years and cobwebs, bears some resemblance to Leonardo's original painting. The hall is empty, the prior and the monks long gone. There is a guide and a booth nearby where booklets are sold, and in the refectory are two photographs showing the effects of a World War II bomb which missed the sandbagged *Last Supper* by only a few yards. The air is still and cool and charged with the overpowering sense of loneliness that one finds in the room of a friend or relative who has died or gone far away. There, no matter what his temperament, a man may find tears in his eyes.

The Last Supper

Through the centuries, since it first began to deteriorate, the wreckage of Leonardo's masterpiece has consistently presented the most difficult problem that experts in restoration have ever faced. The *Last Supper* has been retouched, restored and given up for lost countless times. In 1901 Gabriele D'Annunzio wrote what was considered to be the last of its several epitaphs in his famous *Ode on the Death of a Masterpiece*—"O Poets, it is no longer." However, even as D'Annunzio wrote, restorers equipped with modern skills were preparing one more attempt. A heating system to combat humidity was installed, and during the next 30 years the "skin" of the painting was painstakingly reattached. But just as the restoration began to show promising results, the project director was exiled to a distant province by Mussolini. For 10 years no further work was done, and then the bombing of the monastery destroyed all the restorers' labor.

In 1946 the effort was resumed once more with an astonishing success that may be seen in the detail on the opposite page and in even greater amplification on pages 92 and 93. The painting remains irreparably damaged, but today there appear original colors and details beclouded for centuries—the glow of robes, the series of still lifes on the long table. As one looks at the *Last Supper* in its long historical context, among works ranging in date from the Sixth Century to the 20th *(pages 94-99)*, its pre-eminence as a religious and a human drama is clear beyond all doubt.

In the 1946-1954 restoration, layers of dull paint applied by earlier restorers were removed from Christ's robe, revealing that Leonardo's original color had been flame red, symbolic of the Passion. In the age-darkened landscape, as work progressed, a ribbon of bright blue water appeared.

Christ, detail of *Last Supper*, 1495-1497

Study of an Apostle (probably St. Peter), 1495-1497

Study for Judas, 1495-1497

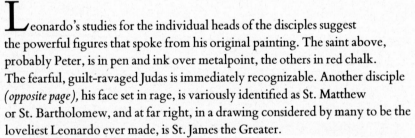

Leonardo's studies for the individual heads of the disciples suggest
the powerful figures that spoke from his original painting. The saint above,
probably Peter, is in pen and ink over metalpoint, the others in red chalk.
The fearful, guilt-ravaged Judas is immediately recognizable. Another disciple
(opposite page), his face set in rage, is variously identified as St. Matthew
or St. Bartholomew, and at far right, in a drawing considered by many to be the
loveliest Leonardo ever made, is St. James the Greater.

In planning the composition as a whole, Leonardo undoubtedly made numerous
studies, but only two of them remain to us today. The more interesting
is the hastily and—for Leonardo—rather carelessly drawn sketch at right. Unable
to place all of his figures at the table because of the small size of the page,
he drew four at the bottom. His intention becomes clear if one visually picks
up the group of four and places it at the left of the upper row—the shoulder
and arm of the disciple at right below are repeated at the extreme left above.
In this preliminary study Leonardo still retains the standard iconography of earlier
Last Suppers—Judas sits alone on the near side of the table.

On the following two pages, with all the clarity and fidelity that
expert restoration, photography and color reproduction can lend it now,
appears the great ruin of the 500-year-old masterpiece itself.

Study, St. Matthew or Bartholomew, 1495-1497

Study for St. James the Greater, 1495-1497

Study for the *Last Supper*, 1495-1497

If the viewer is overwhelmed by the drama of the *Last Supper*—the larger-than-life-sized figures and the compelling variety of their expressive poses—it is sheer revelation to study the individual faces. Second in dominance to Christ, perhaps, is the figure of St. Philip *(opposite page),* who is pictured rising from his seat, and catches the eye because his head is slightly above the others. While Philip touches his breast with both hands as if to protest that he is not the betrayer, St. James the Greater, at his right, stares downward in openmouthed shock. But it is by no means in the figures alone that Leonardo's genius is evident. On the embroidered tablecloth there is a whole sequence of still lifes like that in the detail above, in which wineglasses, pewter dishes and small loaves are placed in a balanced tension that few artists have ever matched.

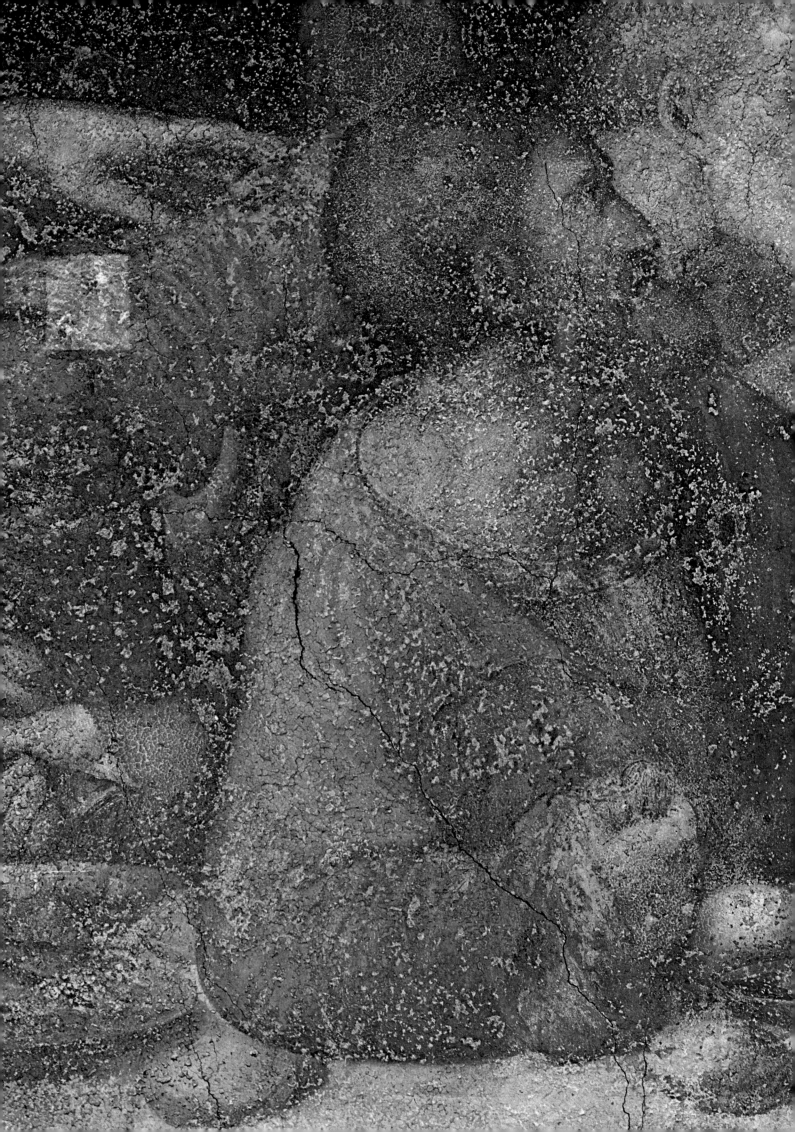

A Miracle of Restoration

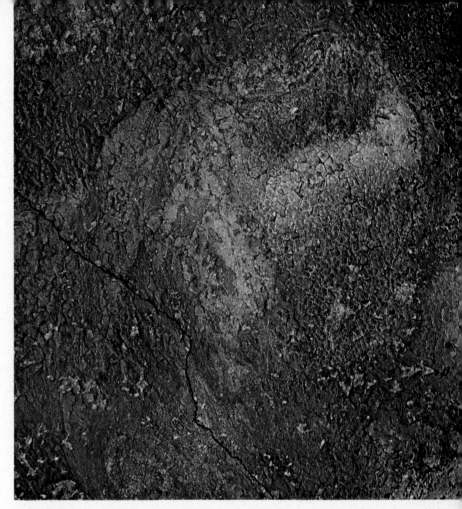

Hand of Judas

Detail of edge of Judas' sleeve

At the end of World War II, the *Last Supper* was in such a perilous state of disintegration that both paint and plaster seemed about to turn to dust. With nothing to lose and everything to gain, Italy's Ministry of Fine Arts made a final attempt to save the painting. A master of restoration, Mauro Pellicioli, set out on an eight-year adventure of exquisitely delicate intellectual and physical work. First, Pellicioli reattached the paint to the wall with a newly developed shellac, absolutely clear and free of wax, with a result that astonished most experts in the field. The colors were not only fixed but seemed to gain new strength—as may be seen in the upper left of the detail on the opposite page, behind the dark head of Judas, where a small rectangle was left to show how the surface appeared before the shellac was applied. This done, Pellicioli gently removed the incrustations of many previous repaintings until he reached what remained of Leonardo's original egg-tempera base for the figures and lime base for the background. At right below, a close-up photograph of 3½ by 4½ inches of Judas' cloak shows the blue areas which have been cleaned, and the brown still covered with old retouching. In the detail of Judas' hand above, the cleaning revealed a change made by Leonardo himself as he worked. The blue tunic sleeve originally covered three fourths of the hand, but was then moved up to wrist length: traces of blue may still be seen on the hand. When Pellicioli completed his work in 1954 there remained nothing further that skill or science could do; the painting, grievously damaged though it was, was at last secure and as close to the original as it could ever be brought.

Judas, detail of *Last Supper*, 1495-1497

Early Christian *Last Supper*, c. 520

Changing Views of the Last Supper

Through all the ages in which the Last Supper has preoccupied Christian artists, one of two dramatic moments has been chosen as the subject: either Christ's institution of Holy Communion, or His statement that one of the disciples would betray Him. In the Early Christian mosaic of the Sixth Century *(above)*, the stress is entirely on Communion—Judas is not singled out, and the figures quietly recline, Roman fashion, at a semicircular table with Christ in the honored position at the left. The late-13th Century Spanish altar frontal *(below)*, for all its liveliness of individual action, again stresses Communion. At the right, however, in a fresco from the School of Pietro Lorenzetti dating from before 1348, the artist has focused on the betrayal—Christ stares at Judas, the only disciple without a halo. And here, extraneous elements in the figures of servants and animals have begun to make their appearance.

Altar frontal of Suriguerola: *Last Supper*, late 13th Century

94

School of Pietro Lorenzetti: *Last Supper*, before 1348

Tintoretto: *Last Supper*, 1591-1594

In the Quattrocento the betrayal of Christ was the moment most commonly chosen for emphasis in the Last Supper, as in Andrea del Castagno's version at the left, completed about 1450. Judas sits isolated, with the strongly mottled panel above his head suggesting a dark sky lanced with thunderbolts. Leonardo doubtless studied this painting as an apprentice, but when he came to create his own masterpiece he filled it with dynamics that Castagno never conceived.

One of the most spectacular treatments of the Last Supper in all art is Tintoretto's, shown below on the opposite page. Painted late in the 16th Century, when the High Renaissance had given way to Mannerism, this version by the great Venetian presents the Last Supper as a night scene, illuminated with supernatural light and reeling with motion—disciples, servants, angels and spectators all seem caught up in a tempest.

In the mid-17th Century the French artist Nicolas Poussin, master of classicism, ignored the betrayal and once again fixed upon the sacrament (below). Although his period was the Baroque, Poussin was a staunch preserver of the earlier tradition—his quiet, three-dimensional figures, reminiscent of Leonardo's or of Raphael's, harmonize with each other in a work unmatched in its sense of spirituality, peace and love.

Andrea del Castagno: *Last Supper*, c. 1450

Nicolas Poussin: *Eucharist*, 1647

Stanley Spencer: *Last Supper,* 1920

In the 18th and 19th Centuries, artists who turned their hands to
the Last Supper seldom achieved the spiritual depth and air of mystery
found in earlier works. However, this feeling has reappeared in
the 20th. The British painter Stanley Spencer, a mystical, imaginative
and deeply religious man, painted his *Last Supper (above)* in 1920, soon
after emerging from combat in World War I. His setting is a malthouse
—the red wall is the side of a grain bin—where common men might
find seclusion for their Communion, and his focal point is the round loaf
which Christ breaks open.

One of the finest of modern presentations of the Last Supper is that
by Emil Nolde at right, completed in 1909. Nolde, a German pioneer
of Expressionism, was keenly sensitive to the suffering of man and
the hope of salvation symbolized in Christ's chalice. The sense
of brotherhood is strongly conveyed with a minimum of homely
gestures—an arm placed around a shoulder, a hand reaching across
to clasp another. Nolde's use of glowing colors is often compared
to that in medieval stained-glass windows; his whole conception
returns, in feeling, to the simplicity and fervor of the Middle Ages.
"I obeyed an irresistible impulse to express deep spirituality and
ardent religious feeling," he wrote. "I painted on and on, scarcely
aware whether it was day or night, whether I was painting or praying."

Emil Nolde: *Last Supper,* 1909

99

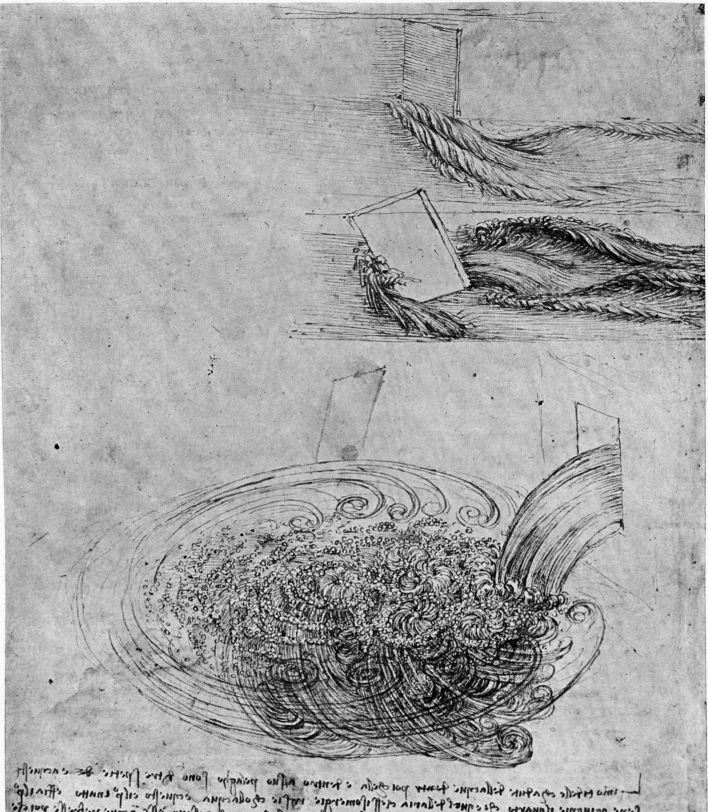

V

Reaching for
the Universe

When Leonardo left Milan after the collapse of Lodovico Sforza's regime he still had within him his last and perhaps his greatest burst of artistic creativity. But now he was nearing 50 and his mind was reaching out toward the furthest boundaries of thought and speculation. The words that Christopher Marlowe's Doctor Faustus spoke of himself applied equally to Leonardo: "Sweet Analytics, 'tis thou hast ravished me!" The scientist was beginning to devour the artist.

A complete evaluation of Leonardo as scientist is impossible—too many of his papers are missing, and the remainder are in such disorder that one cannot trace the evolution of his ideas. His notes, in the two monumental translations by Jean Paul Richter and Edward MacCurdy, have been indexed—under "heat," for example, there are some 50 entries—but with little indication as to what were his tentative and what his final conclusions. The problem is even more difficult because of Leonardo's eclecticism. It is known that he freely borrowed, intact or in altered form, the ideas of his contemporaries. There is, moreover, little written material surviving to indicate precisely what those borrowings may have been, or from what sources.

But some conclusions can be drawn. The first is that Leonardo was by no means the titan of science that some of his more extreme partisans have claimed he was. In at least one instance, because of a single line in his manuscripts, a modern writer credits him with anticipating Copernicus by about 15 years and Galileo by more than a century. The line— "The sun does not move"—does indeed suggest that Leonardo was a revolutionary in rejecting the hallowed idea of an earth-centered universe. But that rejection was first made, after all, by the astronomer Aristarchus of Samos in the Third Century B.C.; the strong probability is that Leonardo, Copernicus and Galileo were all familiar with the writings of that classic scientist.

In the case of Leonardo's celebrated studies for flying machines, his intellectual audacity and thoroughness are beyond question, but it is generally agreed that he spent many years following the wrong track. His methods were sound; he endlessly observed the currents and pressures of

Leonardo's superhuman quickness of vision is shown in these sketches of flowing water—at top, as it swirls around impeding boards, then below as it rushes into a pool. Modern slow-motion films reveal the same patterns he caught (and described in detailed notes) with his unaided eye.

Studies of water formations, c. 1507

air and deduced some of the principles of aerodynamics; he studied the gliding and flapping flights of birds and bats, and anatomized their wings. With his penchant for looking far beyond the immediate fact, he designed devices for use *after* flight had been achieved—a wind-speed indicator; an inclinometer to show the aviator, lost in clouds, whether he was flying level or canted; and what was apparently the world's first parachute, a large pyramidal tent with a light wooden frame. But in his calculations he overlooked the fundamental reason why a man-powered ornithopter cannot rise from the ground in flapping flight. His machines were designed to be driven by the muscles of a man's arms and legs, which together constitute about 22 per cent of his total weight. In birds, the muscles used in flight constitute perhaps 50 per cent of the total. When to this disadvantage one adds the dead weight of the flying machine itself, the difficulty of man-powered flight—at least as Leonardo envisioned it —becomes insuperable. Perhaps eventually an engineer will produce a successful ornithopter, but it will necessarily employ a motor or some other source of power unknown to Leonardo. There is a persistent story that in 1505—after which his notes on flying machines abruptly cease— Leonardo or one of his younger assistants may have made an attempt to fly from the summit of a hill near Florence called Monte Ceceri, but this seems almost certainly a romantic myth.

When the impracticality of man-powered ornithopters was at last— and but recently—realized, Leonardo's partisans could still point to the fact that he had also invented an airscrew or helicopter; his sketches very clearly show one. But his credit for even this has been thrown open to doubt. In the early 1960s, studies of an anonymous 15th Century French painting and of a stained-glass window of about 1525 revealed the Christ Child playing with whirligig toys in which propeller-shaped blades were mounted on spindles wound with cord; a strong pull on the cord would rotate the spindle rapidly enough to send the small "helicopter" rotor soaring upward. Such toys apparently were well known in Leonardo's day; it is possible that his "invention" was merely an adaptation. Only in a single series of sketches, set off in the corner of a large sheet, does Leonardo appear to be driving toward the modern idea of fixed-wing flight. He shows a leaf zigzagging toward the ground, and beneath it four views of a man clinging to a flat winglike surface as he descends through the air. If he had pursued this idea, combining it with his knowledge of wind currents and propulsive forces (he was familiar with powerful springs and it was not beyond his great imagination to hit upon the use of rockets for a jet-assisted takeoff) he might conceivably have launched a successful glider from a mountaintop.

To mention Leonardo's failures, however, is somewhat like blaming Benjamin Franklin for not having invented the electric light. If Leonardo was not a titan he was surely a genius in science, engineering and mechanics; to appreciate this, a brief note about his background may be helpful. During the so-called "Dark" and "Middle" Ages that preceded the Renaissance, scientific progress in Europe had been painfully slow. The environment in which Leonardo found himself resembled a ruined attic, full of the antique furnishings of man's mind, from which he selected what he felt to be worthwhile. It need scarcely be mentioned that for every Toscanelli or Columbus of his time, there were a thousand men who still believed the earth was flat, that the oceans near the equator were boiling hot, that hell existed under the earth and heaven in the empyrean blue, and that the unknown regions of the world were inhabited by all manner of chimerical and human monsters. Over this scene presided the authority of the Church, which, with the best of intentions but often the unhappiest of results, was dedicated to upholding the literal rather than the symbolic truth of every verse in the Bible. Leonardo therefore looked backward to ancient scientists and to their ideas as subtly developed by such Renaissance thinkers as the art theoretician Leon Battista Alberti, the mathematician Fra Luca Pacioli, the physician Marcantonio della Torre and others.

It would require scores of pages to list Leonardo's beliefs and attitudes. However, two or three are worth mentioning. He accepted the Pythagorean ideas that the earth is spherical; that it is composed of the four "elements" of earth, air, fire and water; and that harmonies and proportions are numerically determined. From Plato he accepted the thesis that there is a relationship between man and the universe called the "doctrine of macrocosm and microcosm," by which it is held that the universe, the macrocosm, is a gigantic living organism and that man, the microcosm, is a universe in miniature. Leonardo may have developed some reservations about this in his final years, but meanwhile it led him down some devious byways. "Man has been called by the ancients a lesser world, and indeed the term is well applied," he wrote, "seeing that a man is composed of earth, air, water and fire, and this body of earth is similar. While man has within himself bones as a stay and framework for the flesh, the world has stones which are the support of the earth. While man has within him a pool of blood wherein the lungs as he breathes expand and contract, so the body of the earth has its ocean, which also rises and falls every six hours with the breathing of the world; as from the said pool of blood proceed the veins which spread their branches through the human body, so the ocean fills the body of the earth with an infinite number of veins of water."

Although he was content to accept the Platonic notion of macrocosm and microcosm, Leonardo emphatically rejected Plato's "doctrine of ideas," in which the plain evidence of the senses is denied. Plato and the Neoplatonists of Leonardo's day (the Medici circle, for example) held that because all things are continually changing or subject to change, it is profitless to study an individual object; one ought instead to contemplate the eternal, abstract "idea" of which the object is only a fleeting reflection. Such a concept was contrary to all of Leonardo's thinking; it outraged him. He was first, last and always an artist engrossed in observation of the physical world, and he put limitless trust in vision. "He who loses his sight loses his view of the universe, and is like one interred alive who can still move about and breathe in his grave," he wrote. "Do you not see that the eye encompasses the beauty of the whole world? It is the master of astronomy; it assists and directs all the arts of man. . . . It reigns over the various departments of mathematics, and all its sci-

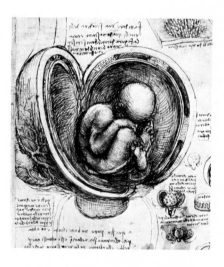

Perhaps the most famous of Leonardo's anatomical drawings is this one of an embryo in the womb. Faulty as it is in some respects, in others—notably the position of the embryo and umbilical cord—it is so accurate and so expertly drawn that it can still be used as an example in medical textbooks today.

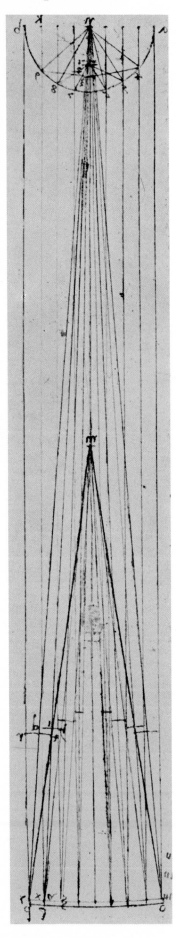

ences are the most infallible." Consequently anyone who suggested to Leonardo da Vinci, of all men, that the evidence of his extraordinarily acute senses was not to be trusted, seemed to him to be either a fool or a charlatan.

When Leonardo used the words "art," "science" and "mathematics" his definitions were somewhat different from those in use today. His beloved mathematics, "the only science which contains within itself its own proof," consisted largely of geometry and proportion. He was absorbed in what could be presented to the eye; the abstractions associated with modern higher mathematics held no particular interest for him. According to Leonardo's definition, art, specifically painting, was a science—actually it was "the Queen of all sciences," which provided not only the means of obtaining knowledge but of "communicating it to all the generations of the world."

His works in art and science are really inseparable. In his *Treatise on Painting,* for example, he may have thought originally of setting down instructions for the correct representation of the physical world, but that soon led to considerations of perspective, proportion, geometry and optics, then to anatomy and the mechanics of both animate and inanimate objects, and ultimately to a search for the mechanics of the universe itself. It was apparently Leonardo's intention to make a compendium of all technical knowledge, even ranging so far as the beginning and end of the world as he imagined them. His method was: 1) close observation, 2) repeated testing of the observation from various viewpoints and 3) drawing the object or phenomenon so skillfully that it would become a "fact" which all the world could see, or could grasp with the aid of brief explanatory notes. Modern scientists object to this "method" on the ground that it is random, empirical and not grounded on sound mathematics or theory. In comparison with the science of Galileo, Newton or Einstein it is weak indeed. However, in certain areas the method enabled Leonardo to present scientific truths or problems in a way that is still unsurpassed, and to make discoveries of great importance, which, unfortunately, remained buried in his notes for centuries.

In the field of botany Leonardo's acute observation made it possible for him to draw plant life so precisely that several of his illustrations could be used with good effect in a botanical textbook of today. By many students he is regarded as the founder of botanical science, which before his time had existed only as a study for pharmacologists and magicians. Leonardo was the first to describe the laws of phyllotaxy, which govern the distribution of leaves; of heliotropism and geotropism, which concern, respectively, the orientation of certain plants toward the sun and the downward growth of roots in response to gravity. He also discovered the possibility of determining the age of plants by studying the structures of their stems, and the age of trees by their annual rings.

In anatomy—a field in which he is held in great esteem—Leonardo was the first to recognize the moderator bands of the right ventricle of the heart, which bear his name, and he originated the technique of drilling pinholes and inserting melted wax into the ventricles of the brain in order to obtain casts of their shapes. He may have been the first to make glass models of organs—it is known that he planned to reproduce in glass the aorta of an ox so that he could observe the passage of blood, and that he proposed to insert a membrane in it to simulate one of the valves. In the hospital of Santa Maria Novella in Florence he performed a dissection which, if it did not involve a discovery, still ranks as unique. During his frequent (and to the patients, perhaps somewhat disconcerting) visits to the hospital he made the acquaintance of a 100-year-old man who was painlessly dying, his symptoms being only weakness and chill. Eventually the old man sat upright, smiled, and "without making another movement or any sign that aught was amiss, passed away from this life." In examining his body to determine the cause of "so gentle a death" Leonardo observed large calcifications in the arteries and wrote a thorough description of them; his report is perhaps the first in medicine that deals in any detail with a death from arteriosclerosis.

In his studies Leonardo dissected the bodies of many animals and made the error—common at the time—of relating their characteristics too closely to those of the human: his famous drawing of an embryo in the uterus shows it with a placental covering more appropriate in a cow than a woman. He was handicapped too by the old idea of macrocosm and microcosm, particularly as it related to the circulation of the blood. He understood arteries and their function; he knew a good deal about the heart and wrote of its pulsations and valves; but he seemed always to be searching for some sort of oceanlike ebb and flow or "flux and reflux," as the ancient physician Galen had put it. It is maddening to pore through his writings, to see him probing all around the periphery of the truth of the circulation of the blood—and failing to make the discovery that was first announced to the world by the British physiologist William Harvey some 100 years later.

Leonardo's great contribution to anatomy lay in the creation of a system of drawing, still in general use, which enabled physicians to transmit their findings to students. Prior to his time the medical profession took small interest in anatomical drawing; indeed, many physicians actually opposed its use in books as distracting from the text. Leonardo's system involved the presentation of four views of a subject, so that the observer might in effect walk completely around it; and this was at once so clear and effective that physicians could no longer deny the value of art in teaching. He also introduced the technique of cross-sectional representation and achieved wonderfully clear "transparencies" of systems of veins, arteries and nerves. With the appearance of the first "modern" medical textbook, the *De humanis corporis fabrica* of Vesalius (1543), which was illustrated with woodcuts based on Leonardo's method, anatomical drawing became what it is today.

In his view of the cosmos Leonardo was again hampered by the antique but persistent notion of the elements of earth, air, fire and water. He did appear to believe that the earth revolves around the sun, and he described the latter in words that might have been written fairly recently: "The sun has substance, shape, movement, radiance, heat and generative power; and these qualities all emanate from itself without its diminution." He also had a clear idea of the insignificance of the earth

. . . as described by Leonardo

Whether he was studying human anatomy or optical theory, Leonardo's scientific method was a combination of experiment and deduction. His detailed explanation of the aberrations of a concave spherical mirror is translated below. On the opposite page is his accompanying diagram. Reference points are identified in his characteristic mirror writing.

In respect of concave mirrors of the same diameter, the one with least concavity will unite a greater number of rays at the focal point of the said rays, and as a result will kindle fire the more readily and strongly.

Let the arc o p represent the mirror mentioned above; let a b be the locus between rays, raining down from the sun onto the mirror; n marks the center of the circle of the sphere, from which the said mirror gets its concavity; m is the point where most of the reflected rays converge, and where greater heat can be produced than in any other part of the pyramid of rays o p m.

The line or ray of sun that falls from b to p is that reflected in the line p m, at equal angles, as can be measured by the arc t r on the circumference round the point or center p. The same happens to all the rays that come from the sun a b, always striking the mirror and being reflected back from it at equal angles, as shown in the angles v x.

within the universe. After noting that although distant stars appear small he pointed out that many are much greater in size than the earth, and added, "Think, then, what this star of ours would seem like at so great a distance, and then consider how many stars might be set longitudinally and latitudinally amid these stars which are scattered throughout this dark expanse." For his astronomical studies Leonardo built an observatory of some sort, which his notes leave tantalizingly undescribed. Even more tantalizing is his instruction to himself, "Make glasses in order to see the moon large." He was familiar with the construction and function of lenses; did he intend to insert them in a tube to make the world's first telescope?

In geology Leonardo's most significant contribution was his correct explanation of the marine fossils found in the mountains of Italy: he concluded that all places where such fossils are found must once have been covered by the primeval oceans. The idea was contrary to the teaching of the Church, which held that land and sea were separated by God on the third day of creation more than 3,000 years ago. A compromise explanation of marine fossil remains was that they had been deposited during the Deluge, but Leonardo relentlessly (if only in the privacy of his notes) knocked this down. Fossils are found in different geological layers, he wrote, indicating with irrefutable logic not one but successive inundations. The whole concept of a universal Flood struck him as ridiculous. "We have it in the Bible," he noted, "that the said Flood . . . rose ten cubits above the highest mountain in the world," thus creating a sphere of water incapable of motion, since water does not move except to descend. "How then did the waters of so great a Flood depart if it is proved that they have no power of motion? If it departed, how did it move unless it went upward? At this point natural causes fail us, and therefore, in order to resolve such a doubt, we must needs either call in a miracle to our aid or else say that all this water was evaporated by the heat of the sun."

In his reflections on fossils Leonardo borrowed Ovid's description of the passage of time, but altered it for his own purposes. His description of his thoughts on a fossilized fish, even in translation, has something of the majesty of Herman Melville and indicates Leonardo's prose style at its best. "O Time, swift despoiler of created things! How many kings, how many peoples hast thou brought low! How many changes of state and circumstance have followed since the wondrous form of this fish died here in this hollow, winding recess? Now destroyed by Time, patiently it lies in this narrow space, and with its bones despoiled and bare, it has become armor and support to the mountain which lies above it."

In his studies of fossils Leonardo was accurate and apparently original in describing the formation of sedimentary rocks; but oddly—in a part of the world notable for volcanic and earthquake activity—the igneous and metamorphic held little interest for him. He believed that the forces of water had shaped the world and would ultimately destroy it; indeed he was persuaded that the Mediterranean was an enormous river which runs "from the source of the Nile to the Western ocean."

With his interest in all that can be observed by the eye, Leonardo went

Leonardo's water shoes probably never got beyond the rough sketch shown here, but there is no doubt that they would have worked—after a fashion. In modern versions, buoyant shoes and balancing sticks have been manufactured, but more for fun than transportation.

deeply into the subject of optics. He understood that images are reversed on the human retina, and he is credited by many with the invention of the camera obscura. Optical illusions intrigued him, and for some he gave explanations still in use: from a distance a brightly lit object appears larger than an identical object dimly lit; in discussing reflection he noted, in precisely the terms used by a modern teacher of physics, that "the angle of incidence is always equal to the angle of reflection." In sketching an instrument to measure the intensity of light, he drew a photometer as practical as that "invented" by the American-born scientist Benjamin Rumford three centuries later. In his innumerable studies of shadows he worked out the phenomenon of umbra and penumbra; he was familiar with eyeglasses and in his old age apparently made and used them; he explained accurately that the iridescence in the plumage of certain birds, or in patches of oil on a wet surface, is caused by the refraction of light rays. But in almost all of these instances Leonardo was content to carry his observations, if a weak but appropriate pun may be permitted, no further than the eye could see. He did not codify, formulate or arrive at all-encompassing principles.

Perhaps the most interesting of Leonardo's few attempts to define such principles may be found in his studies of basic mechanics. He came exceedingly close to formulating Newton's first law of motion, that of inertia, which holds that a body at rest will remain at rest unless some outside force is applied to it, and that, as a corollary, a body in motion will continue to move unless an agency such as friction causes it to halt. Leonardo did not make his formulation in a single sentence or paragraph, but the concept is undeniably present in his scattered notes. In one manuscript can be found: "Nothing whatever can be moved by itself, but its motion is effected through another. This other is the force." Elsewhere Leonardo wrote that "all movement tends to maintenance, or rather all moved bodies continue to move as long as the impression of the force of their motors (original impetus) remains in them." It would be extravagant to claim that Leonardo anticipated Newton's *Principia* other than in this respect, but it is true that the principle of inertia was called the principle of Leonardo for many years.

This life preserver conceived by Leonardo was an eminently practical invention. What material he meant to use for buoyancy is not known, but the counterpart of his conception was later to become traditional on shipboard in the form of a cork ring covered with canvas.

To Leonardo, "mechanics is the paradise of the mathematical sciences because by means of it one comes to the fruits of mathematics." Apart from his studies of flight, it is in his mechanical work, as engineer, inventor and (in no demeaning sense) gadgeteer that his popular fame as "scientist" principally rests. Whatever his lack of method, and whatever the incongruity of his temporary diversion from some tremendous work of art in order to design, for example, a self-closing privy lid, it seems true that no mechanician in history has approached him in breadth of interest and ingenuity. Some of his inventions were impractical from the moment he conceived them; some were beyond the technical capacities of the Renaissance to produce; one or two can only be described as pre-Rube Goldberg. An idea of their range can best be suggested in the brief catalogue that follows.

Leonardo, although he was moderate in his habits to the point of asceticism, did not believe in long sleep, which he regarded as the younger brother of death. Before the invention of reliable timepieces with alarm attachments, he described a hilarious contrivance to wake him: it involved the slow drip of water from an upper into a lower vessel which, when full, operated a lever that jerked his feet upward. To magnify the force of the lever he employed what is now known as a "mechanical relay," by which a small force is increased—"and this force being doubled," he noted, "jerks violently upward the feet of the sleeper, who is thus awakened and goes about his business."

If the foregoing shows the great man in a playful mood, his studies of power transmission certainly do not. He drew many sketches of pulleys in various combinations, indicating the mechanical advantage to be gained from each. He was also fascinated by the possibilities of multiplying forces through gearing; one of his sketches shows three cogwheels of ascending diameter meshing with a "lantern" or conical gear, by means of which increasing speeds of rotation can be obtained. The system is quite similar to the variable-speed drive that was until recently used in most automobiles. Obviously he could have had no thought of applying it to cars, although he did design a spring-driven "automobile" *(page 114)* which, if it had been constructed, might have been able to travel a few rods over level ground.

Leonardo also used gearing in a highly ingenious manner in his drawing of a mechanical spit for turning meat over a fire. His plan was to insert a fan-shaped rotor, to be turned by rising currents of heated air, inside a chimney. The rotor was attached by a long rod to a set of gears, from which the power was transmitted to the turnspit by belting, possibly of metal. The hotter the fire, the faster the spit turned, thus preventing the meat from being charred as it might have been if cooked by an inattentive servant. In another of his drawings chain belting appears: the joined links very much resemble those to be seen in a modern bicycle. Apparently Leonardo was content to conceive the links but put them to no practical use—they seem first to have been employed in France in 1832.

A man well acquainted with workshop operations, Leonardo invented a mechanical saw in which the straight blade moved vertically, and to the treadle-operated lathe of the time he added a heavy flywheel, perhaps the first in all mechanics, to provide steady and continuous motion. After observing the then-current boring machines, which were used to turn tree trunks into water pipes, Leonardo made what cannot be called an invention, but was certainly a massive application of common sense. Customarily the tree trunks, secured vertically in place, were bored from the top downward, with the result that chips accumulated in the bore and fouled the bit. Leonardo sketched a machine which bored upward, with a conical shield to protect the operator against the rain of chips that naturally fell down out of the hole. He also invented a machine that combined the punching-out of blanks and the die-stamping of coins, and another in which sheets of paper, ordinarily hand-fed into the screw-type printing presses of his day, were automatically injected. As civil engineer he was master of the construction of canals, locks and weir gates; he also proposed a workable (though to his contemporaries, laughable) method of lifting a great stone building through the use of jacks, and in his preoccupation with the construction of canals he designed dredges and cranes and earth-moving equipment of extraordinary capacity for the time.

To the modern speculative mind, Leonardo's experiments with steam are a source of wonder and frustration, like his near-miss in the case of blood circulation. He began, evidently, with the construction (perhaps invention) of a calorimeter to measure the volume of steam produced by the boiling of a given quantity of water. A sketch of his device shows, very likely for the first time in science or mechanics, a piston moving within a cylinder. He also proposed a steam gun, which he called an "architronito," in which a sudden blast of steam, admitted by valve into the barrel, would drive the projectile (i.e., the piston) about half a mile. He must therefore have understood the use of steam as a motive power, although there is no indication whatever that he had any conception of the steam engine as such. But speculation is persistent as to what his influence may have been on its development. In 1956 the Milanese engineer Ladislao Reti published a fascinating paper in which he set forth the idea that Leonardo's unpublished notes were available, at least to certain men, not long after his death. (This much is demonstrably true.) Reti then goes on to trace the development of the steam engine by various men during many years and finds enough coincidences between their notes and Leonardo's to intrigue the most skeptical of men. There the matter must rest—a trifle uneasily.

The catalogue of Leonardo's inventions, ideas and adaptations might be extended indefinitely: light, ski-like "shoes" for walking on water, such as have been marketed in the U.S. in recent years; webbed gloves as swimming aids; a revolving wind cowl for chimneys; rolling mills for producing thin, uniform sheets of metal; an improved centrifugal pump; machines for making metal screws; the idea of prefabricated portable houses; rope-making and grinding machines; experiments with spinning tops, liquids, falling bodies; an oil lamp fitted with a glass globe filled with water to magnify its light.

In considering Leonardo's staggering quantity and range of accomplishments in science and technology, it is all too easy to be overawed. His habit of borrowing from others must constantly be borne in mind. It was not plagiarism—his intent, as mentioned, was to make a sort of encyclopedia of knowledge that can be visually transmitted. It requires a very judicious mind, as well as a vast knowledge of Renaissance science which few men possess—to avoid giving Leonardo too little credit or, as some would do, too much. Leonardo himself seems to have tended in the latter direction. His accomplishments were great and real, but he wanted credit for even more. When he was engrossed in anatomy he wrote a note mentioning the talents required for that science—and mentioning also a volume of writing so large that he could scarcely have completed it. "Concerning [these talents], whether or no they have all been found in me, the hundred and twenty books which I have composed will give their verdict 'yes' or 'no.' In these I have not been hindered by avarice or negligence but only by want of time. Farewell!"

The Man of Science

The term "Renaissance Man" brings to mind Leonardo above all others—none of his contemporaries, brilliant and many-sided though they were, approached him in intellectual range. The mere catalogue of his nonartistic pursuits seems almost beyond credence: anatomy, botany, cartography, geology, mathematics, aeronautics, optics, mechanics, astronomy, hydraulics, sonics, civil engineering, weaponry, city planning.

With such a range of interests, why does not Leonardo emerge as one of the greatest scientific geniuses of all time? The answer is that while he was a creative man of science, he was so only to a degree. He had a scientist's vast curiosity about nature's secrets, and what he learned he applied to his scientific investigations. The meticulousness of his drawings indicates, furthermore, that he harbored at least the thought of putting his ideas into practice. But he never did; Leonardo always seemed to go on to other things before he took the final step of bringing his projects to concrete, functioning reality. His notes and drawings remained his own secret; he did not allow them to be examined, tested or put to use. And herein lies the reason for his lack of success as a scientist, for in the last analysis the achievements of the inventive man of science must be judged in the practical world—with which the solitary Leonardo had only such dealings as he found necessary, otherwise preferring to remain aloof.

Leonardo's cross section of the interior of the skull was the first in the history of anatomy. His notes refer to "the confluence of all the senses" at the intersection of the diagonal and vertical lines—mistakenly he believed that all sensations, especially the "emanations" of vision, converged here.

Anatomical drawing of a skull facing left, 1489

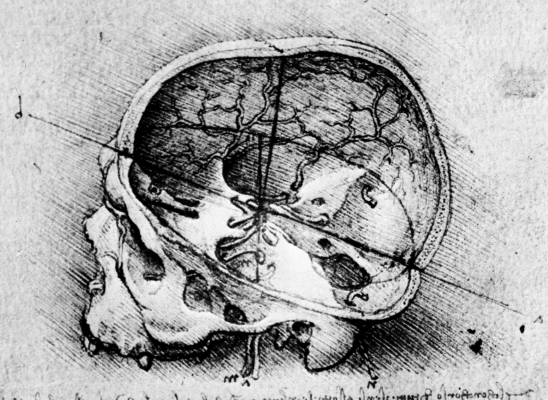

Volcanic eruption, date uncertain

In his studies of geology Leonardo took the view that the forces of water and tempest were of primary importance in molding the earth, and he made extraordinarily penetrating and accurate deductions concerning fossils and the formation of sedimentary rock. However, although it is known that he had information about Mt. Etna, he had small interest in igneous rock formation—in his papers there is only one abstract drawing of a volcanic eruption *(left)*, with no accompanying comment.

As a maker of maps Leonardo soared immeasurably far

Map of Northern Italy showing the watershed of the Arno, c. 1502

above his time. The cartographers of the Quattrocento customarily presented views seen from a particular spot, sometimes drawing small pictures of themselves on the map to indicate precisely where that spot was. Leonardo, in contrast, combined his knowledge of scientific perspective, his imagination and his art to produce such wonders as the map of Tuscany *(below, left)*. In making it, he postulated a then-impossible viewpoint, high in space above the hills and streams. Along the bottom may be seen the coast of the Tyrrhenian Sea and above it the Arno River and its watersheds. The elevations are indicated, exactly as on the maps in a modern atlas, by gradations in color from green to dark brown.

The drawing of oak leaves and acorns *(below)*, a single sheet among many which record his interest in plant life, suggests how he was able to discover several fundamental botanical principles. His "method" was visual observation so incredibly acute that he could not only record vital details previously missed by others, but also capture in his drawings the sense of life and growth within the plant.

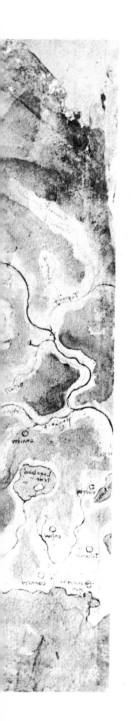
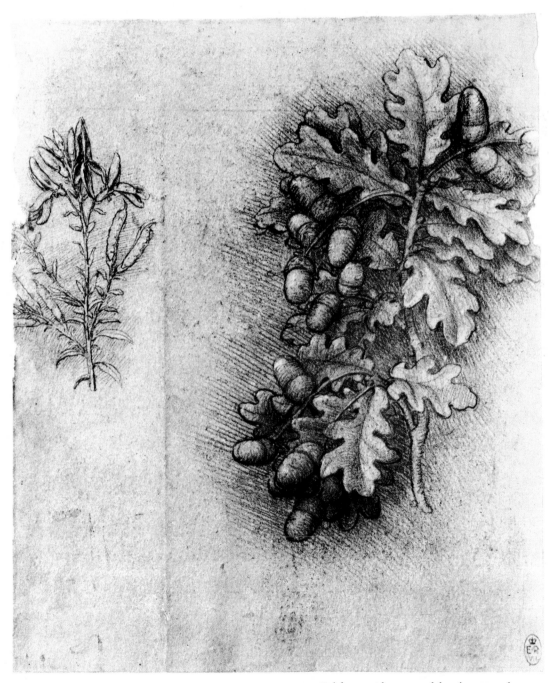

Oak leaves with acorns and dyers' greenweed, c. 1505

113

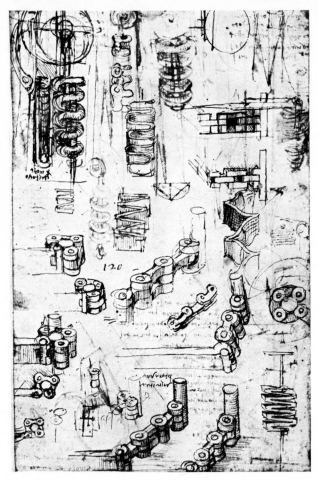

Chain links, c. 1490

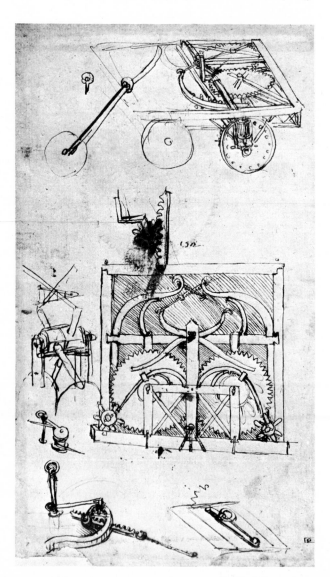

Leonardo's applied mechanics, perhaps more than any other of his scientific or technical pursuits, strike sparks of recognition and admiration in the machine-conscious 20th Century mind. Many of his inventions, such as the chain links *(left, above),* can be understood at a glance. With only brief study, modern craftsmen have produced working models of his spring-driven car and his flyer spindle. The car *(left)* is designed to be propelled by two sets of curved springs which release their power alternately; while one set is at work, the operator cranks up the other, and thus continuous motion is obtained. The flyer spindle *(right)* is similar in principle to those used in the textile machinery of today. The flyer is the wishbone-shaped part: Leonardo's ingenious gearing causes it not only to rotate but also to move back and forth, winding the thread evenly on the spool.

Mechanical car, c. 1490

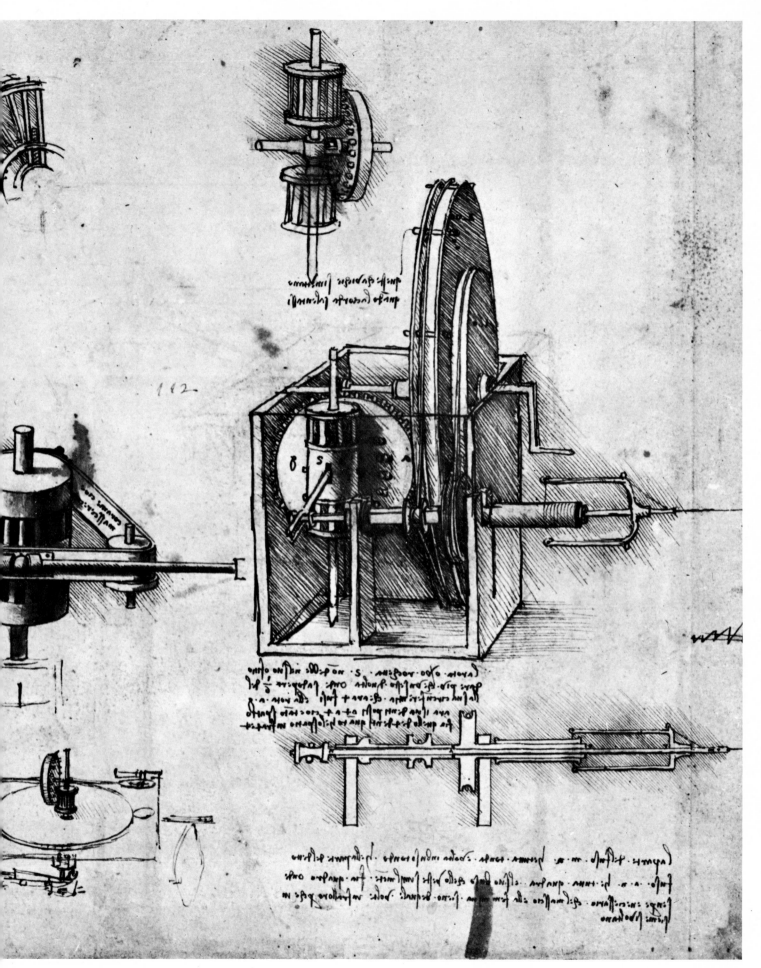

Spinning wheel, c. 1490

Airscrew, c. 1488

Artificial flight was a riddle which obsessed Leonardo: he labored on its solution for about 25 years. He approached it, as he did his other investigations, with what is as a rule a sound premise: "Although human subtlety makes a variety of inventions . . . it will never devise an invention more beautiful, more simple or more direct than does nature, because in her inventions nothing is lacking and nothing is superfluous." Unhappily for him, the secret of motive power forever eluded him, and thus his prolonged efforts to imitate the flight of birds came to nothing. In the main he concentrated on designs for flapping flights such as that on the opposite page in which a man lying prone on a board is intended to

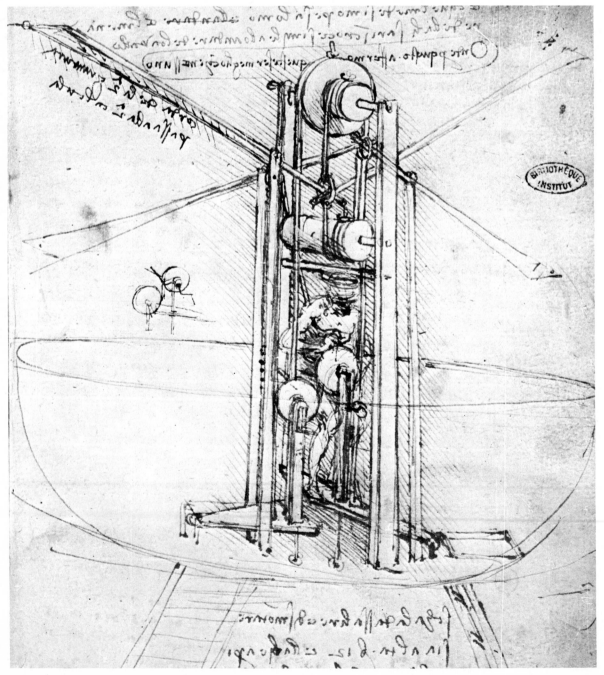

Flying machine with a man operating it, c. 1488

manipulate wings. Occasionally his obsession led him to strange extremes—the contrivance with twin sets of paddles and bowl-shaped fuselage at left below is perhaps the least sound design he ever made. However, several of his ideas were brilliant. The pyramidal parachute would doubtless have been successful, and it may be that Leonardo was the first inventor in history to conceive such a device. Of greatest interest to aeronautical engineers today is his design for a helical airscrew (top left). Leonardo evidently thought it minor and may have derived the idea from whirligig toys invented by others. Nonetheless, many scientists regard it as the first helicopter and the precursor of the modern propeller.

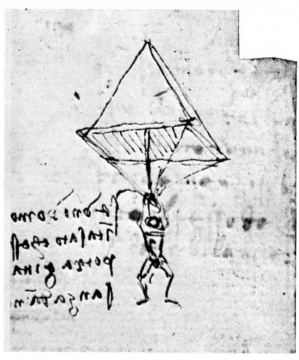

Parachute, c. 1490

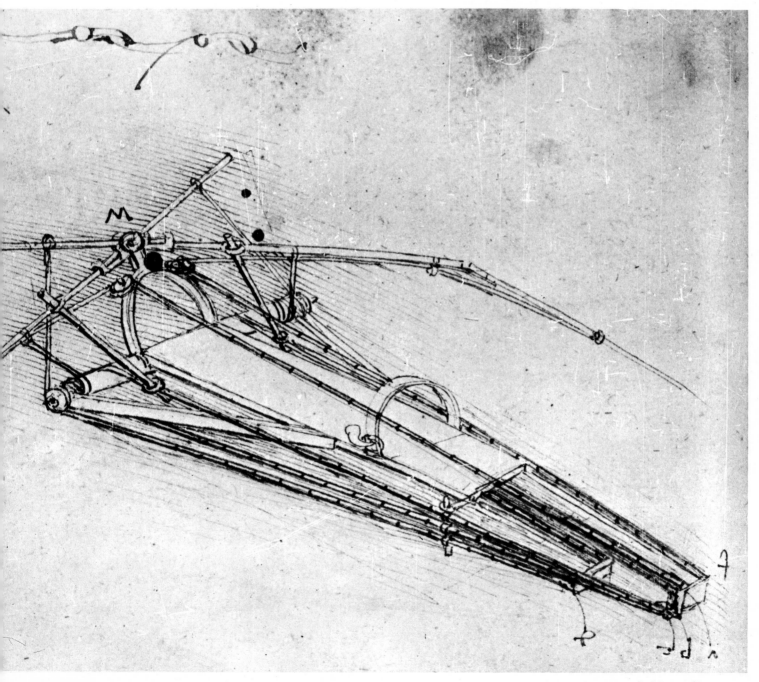

Drawing of a flying machine, c. 1488

VI

A Sunburst of Greatness

Leonardo's brief, impersonal comments about the downfall of Milan, his home for 18 years, may seem disconcertingly cool but they merely reveal what was true. Like many solitary men of genius he had no strong sense of attachment to any political institution or locality; his real nation lay within himself. The end of Sforza meant simply that Leonardo would have to find a new source of patronage; it was a bother. However, by 1499, as the creator of *The Horse* and the *Last Supper,* his reputation was such that he did not have to go begging.

His plan was to return to Florence, but he went there circuitously, stopping first in the city of Mantua, where he studied the frescoes of Andrea Mantegna. There he encountered an intelligent but stupefyingly insistent woman, the marchioness Isabella d'Este, sister-in-law of Sforza. Nothing would do but that Leonardo should paint her portrait, and she set about hounding him with all the wiles at her command. Her powers of persuasion, cajolery and threat were formidable—as notable an artist as the Venetian Giovanni Bellini, who had no desire to produce a painting for her, had earlier capitulated. Even Leonardo, who could almost always turn aside tedious requests by overawing or dazzling those who made them, was able to resist Isabella only in part. Early in 1500 he was driven so far as to make a cartoon of her in profile. (In painting, "cartoon" has no satirical or comic-strip connotations. It means a full-sized, detailed study on paper, which is later to be transferred or copied on a permanent surface.)

The cartoon, which is probably the one now in the Louvre, has been heavily touched up and is insignificant in Leonardo's total work. In looking at it, however, one cannot resist the speculation that Leonardo, as he drew, was taking his revenge on that aggressive woman. Even if he had been so inclined, it is doubtful that he would have caricatured her—she was, after all, the wife of the marquis and therefore too powerful to insult. What he apparently did was to draw her with pitiless accuracy: dull of face, fairly homely, flabby-chinned. But even this did not discourage her. She continued to pressure Leonardo for years thereafter, trying to extract from him a permanent portrait in color, or, indeed, any painting at all. She never got one. However, she has some small importance in his history;

the letters sent back to her by her emissaries, while gently hinting of his unwillingness to serve her, reveal a few details of Leonardo's career that might otherwise be unknown.

Departing from Mantua, no doubt with relief, Leonardo then went to Venice. His sojourn there was brief—perhaps three months—but he had considerable impact on Venetian art, or at least on that of the High Renaissance master Giorgione, who was then only 22 and still developing his style. The biographer Vasari notes of Giorgione that "having seen some things of Leonardo delicately and deeply modeled with dark shadows, they pleased him so much that as long as he lived he made them his models, and in oil painting imitated them greatly." Giorgione was far too great a painter to have become in any sense an imitator of Leonardo. But his works reflect contact with Leonardo's art not only in certain specific motifs (for example, in his *Christ Bearing the Cross* in San Rocco, Venice) but in his basic conception of plastic, three-dimensional forms.

Leonardo's reputation as an artist had not alone preceded him to Venice. He was known, too, as a military engineer, and at the time of his arrival the Venetians had great need of one. Among the Italian city-states Venice had done more venturing and trading eastward than any other; her sea power had brought her into conflict with the maritime ambitions of the Sultan of Turkey who now, by land and water, was assaulting Venetian territories with Levantine ferocity. The Turkish spahis were burning the nearby countryside; at night their fires could be seen from the campanile of St. Mark's, and by day their sharkish galleys, filled with archers, cruised close inshore. Whether Leonardo volunteered his services to the Venetians, or whether he was formally retained, is not clear. He did, however, make a topographical study of the land roundabout, and concluded that in order to reach Venice itself, the Sultan's troops would have to cross the Isonzo River. He recommended the construction of a dam with floodgates which might be opened to drown the invaders, and then turned his attention to the destruction of the Turkish fleet. To this end he devised diving suits and what seems to have been a small submarine, so that the ships might be approached underwater and sunk. These were not new ideas—Aristotle had written about the diving bell, and Leonardo had at hand descriptions of the masks and breathing tubes used by Oriental pearl divers. However, he may well have invented a novel scheme of supplying air to a man underwater. Whatever this was, he refused to divulge its secret, "on account of the evil nature of men." One's inclination is to doubt—on other occasions, Leonardo was eager enough to demonstrate horrendous weapons. But his cryptic notes, plus his written advice to himself to "choose a simple youth" to help in the private manufacture of his diving equipment, suggest that he was on the track of something extraordinary.

As his plans burgeoned, Leonardo became euphoric. He was so certain that he would demolish the Turks that, daydreaming, he wrote flamboyant notes—"I will destroy the harbor! Unless you surrender within four hours, you will go to the bottom!" He also composed letters demanding a large share of the booty to be obtained from the yet-undefeated fleet—"one half of the ransom to be yours without deduction," and attempted to set up arrangements to make sure the Venetians could not cheat him out

Isabella d'Este, the willful, persistent marchioness who for so long pressed Leonardo to paint her portrait, received only this drawing made in Mantua, after the artist left Milan in 1500. Done in black chalk, charcoal and pastel, its fine lines were blurred by a later hand.

of his due. But the upshot of his adventure was zero. Leonardo for some reason left the city, and the Venetians got rid of the Turks without his help. The affair is an enigma, another of the insoluble puzzles of his life.

When he arrived in Florence in the spring of 1500 Leonardo found an atmosphere wholly changed. Five hundred years earlier, at the approach of the year 1000—the Millennium—the Christian world had been convulsed by an outburst of religious fervor which in places verged on madness; the end of the world, as darkly suggested in the Book of Revelations, was thought to be at hand. Now in Florence, as another great round-numbered year approached, something similar though not nearly so extensive had taken place. Lorenzo the Magnificent was dead; without his skills the Medici family had lost their grip on Florence and had been expelled. During the 1490s the fanatic Dominican monk Savonarola had deeply stirred the people with thunderous prophecies of impending doom. "Down, down with all gold and decorations, down where the body is food for the worms!" he cried, and caused the guilt-stricken Florentines to build an enormous bonfire in which ornaments, rich costumes, manuscripts and paintings were consumed. Ultimately the people turned against him; in 1498 he was hanged and then burned in the Piazza della Signoria. Two years later, when Leonardo returned, an air of gloom still lingered.

Leonardo, who disliked what he knew of Savonarola, could scarcely have been affected by his dire predictions and death, but he may have been depressed by what he saw in the field of art. Much of the spontaneity and gaiety of the Quattrocento had perished. Botticelli and Filippino Lippi had forsaken their "pagan" style and turned to religious themes. Of the other artists Leonardo had known in his youth, his master Verrocchio had long been dead; Ghirlandaio and Antonio del Pollaiuolo too were in their graves. The great rising favorite was the 25-year-old Michelangelo, whose reputation already rivaled that achieved by Leonardo at 48.

The returning master was treated with the deference he deserved. The Servite monks of the Annunziata commissioned him to paint an altarpiece and gave him private quarters in their monastery into which Leonardo and his household, including the young Salai, presently moved. Ordinarily the monks might have assigned him a specific subject—during the Renaissance it was rare for an artist to undertake a painting on his own account and then attempt to locate a patron or purchaser; rather, he awaited instructions, which often included not only the subject but the shape and measurements of the painting-to-be. However, in this case Leonardo had been working independently on a major theme even before the Servites approached him, and in their awe they were apparently content to give him a free hand. The theme he had begun to develop was that of the Virgin and Child with the Virgin's mother, St. Anne, on which he would labor at intervals for at least 15 years—his last statement of it is an unfinished painting *(page 139)* made long after he left the Servites. The first phase may be seen in the so-called *Burlington House Cartoon,* recently purchased by the British government and now in the National Gallery in London *(page 138).* Leonardo made the cartoon around 1499, and probably showed it to the monks to suggest what he might produce for them.

In the first instant of glancing at the cartoon, one senses, apart from its extraordinary beauty, that there is something very unusual about it —and then realization dawns: Leonardo has accomplished a prodigious feat of composition. He has placed one full-grown woman seated on the lap of another. If one transposes this arrangement to everyday life, it becomes ridiculous. But in the cartoon the composition arouses nothing but admiration. Two gracious women, supposedly mother and daughter but mysteriously equal in age, are poised in a wonderful balance of weight and mass, communing with gentle, flickering expressions. Binding them together is the body of the Christ Child, twisting to bless the infant John the Baptist at the right. This cartoon, perfect in its plastic rendering and depth of emotional expression, strikes many admirers of Leonardo as the most satisfying of all his works. Nonetheless, he did not find it good enough; having achieved a stable harmony, he abandoned it, and set out to make a more dynamic arrangement.

The second version of the theme was another cartoon—the one produced for the Servites—which has been lost. There are only literary remains. "When it was finished," wrote Vasari, "the chamber wherein it stood was crowded for two days by men and women, old and young; a concourse, in short, such as one sees flocking to the most solemn festivals, all hastening to behold the wonders produced by Leonardo." The showing took place in March or April 1501, as indicated in a letter written to Isabella d'Este by one of her emissaries. Leonardo had replaced John the Baptist with a lamb, and, as the emissary noted, "these figures are life-sized but they are in a small cartoon because all are seated or bent, and each one is placed before the other, to the left."

Delighted and hopeful as the Servites may have been at the appearance of their cartoon and the public reaction to it, they were not destined to get a finished painting from Leonardo—then, or ever. Isabella's messenger reported that he appeared to have lost interest in art—"the sight of a brush puts him out of temper." This seems temporarily to have been the case; Leonardo abruptly left the Servites, and for about eight months in 1502 and 1503 he again took service as a military engineer. His employer was no relatively mild despot such as Lodovico Sforza—it was Cesare Borgia, the most cruel, ruthless and perfidious tyrant of the Renaissance.

C esare was one of several illegitimate children of Pope Alexander VI, a venal, lecherous man who assumed the papacy in the memorable year 1492. He made Cesare a Cardinal at 17, but life in the Vatican was not quite suitable to the young man. His character may be judged in some degree by the legends he inspired—on one occasion, he stabbed to death an enemy who was standing so close to his father that blood splashed on the papal robes; while on another, he assembled some condemned prisoners in a courtyard of the palace and, as the Pope and another of his illegitimate children, the ill-famed Lucrezia Borgia, looked on, entertained himself by shooting the hapless, dodging victims in whatever parts of their bodies he found amusing to hit with his arrows. The Pope, remarking that Cesare did not seem cut out for the spiritual life, released him from his vows and set about making him lord of the Romagna, an amorphous area in north-central Italy, lying between Tuscany and the Adriatic, to which the Papal States had claim.

Cesare Borgia was more northern than Mediterranean in appearance, and there is good reason to believe that this red-chalk drawing by Leonardo is a portrait of the fearsome *condottiere*. Leonardo's rendering of the curly, light-colored beard, similar to that known to have been affected by Cesare, supports this conclusion.

It was during his conquest of the Romagna and neighboring areas in 1502 that Cesare summoned Leonardo as architect and engineer-in-chief. Leonardo accepted the assignment, despite the common knowledge of Cesare's character and methods. Cesare gave Leonardo a letter of carte blanche, instructing his subordinates in the conquered territories to give Leonardo full information about all fortifications and to follow his instructions for improvement. Leonardo's first assignment seems to have been at the Mediterranean coastal city of Piombino, already in Cesare's hands, where he designed a system of ditches and canals to drain the pestiferous and foul-smelling marshes. Apparently he spent much time observing the crashing and retirement of the waves along the shore—he sketched them, referred to them in his notes, and in part they may have formed the basis of his later, cataclysmic drawings and description of the end of the world. Soon after Leonardo journeyed to Arezzo, a satellite city of Florence, and drew maps to aid Borgia's forces in an attack upon his fellow Tuscans.

Leonardo was with Cesare when the Duchy of Urbino was taken by characteristic Borgian treachery. Cesare approached his friend, the Duke of Urbino, and asked for the loan of some artillery for a campaign elsewhere. The trusting Duke obliged—and immediately had to flee for his life when he found himself menaced by his own weapons turned against him. If Leonardo was surprised or shocked by this, he made no note of it. Instead he drew a ground plan of the fortress of Urbino and of a dovecote whose beauty impressed him.

In Urbino Leonardo made the acquaintance of the famous—and much-maligned—Niccolò Machiavelli, who was serving as an emissary from the Florentine republic to Borgia. Leonardo and Machiavelli, drawn together by their qualities of intellect and keen observation, soon became close friends. They accompanied Cesare on his campaigns during the summer and fall of 1502, Leonardo making maps, sketches for canals, a novel windmill and another ideal city plan, while Machiavelli studied Borgia and made mental notes for the book he was later to write, *The Prince*.

Doubtless at this time Machiavelli came to some conclusions about the military conduct of Italian city-states. Their armies as a rule were composed of mercenaries led by *condottieri*—free-lance generals, strong of body and personality, who recruited troops among the peasants, paying them more than they could earn in the groves and vineyards and throwing in the promise of booty and an occasional rape. The *condottieri* were notoriously unreliable; they would fight for the highest bidder, often switching sides on the eve of combat, and they followed what amounted to union rules: no fighting during the cold of winter, much shouting but little bloodshed, and gentlemanly treatment of fellow professionals, although of no one else.

Cesare had difficulties with his own *condottieri*—once they turned openly against him and besieged him in the city of Imola, at which time Leonardo may have made the red-chalk studies of him which still exist. But Cesare extricated himself and—on the surface—patched up his differences with them. However, he was merely preparing for his master stroke. In December 1502, he convinced his "dear brothers" that they had nothing to fear from him and persuaded four of them to attend a banquet at Sinigaglia. There, separated from their troops, they were easy prey. Two of them were strangled on the spot, and two sent as prisoners to Rome, where they were later murdered.

Machiavelli and Leonardo were probably both present at Sinigaglia, although they did not witness the murders. Conceivably this affair at last alienated Leonardo—one of the strangled men, Vitellozzo Vitelli, had been his friend. At any rate, Leonardo soon thereafter left Cesare's service and in the spring of 1503 was back in Florence. As for Borgia himself, his fortunes steadily declined after 1503 when the death of his father, the Pope, deprived him of his principal support, and in 1507 he was killed for his valuable armor in a minor skirmish.

These two studies show Leonardo's mastery of the male nude. Done in red chalk and pen and ink, they also reveal how deeply impressed he was with Michelangelo's handling of the male figure. At the time Leonardo drew them, he was working on his *Battle of Anghiari* (a sketch for which is visible here), and Michelangelo was painting his *Battle of Cascina* on another wall of the same room.

The question of why Leonardo, whose gentleness Vasari so strongly emphasizes, should have involved himself with Borgia is one that may be more suitably treated in a discussion of his character. But a brief note about Machiavelli, one of the great figures of the world of Leonardo, cannot easily be omitted. His *Prince,* which seems to many readers a manual of wickedness and has caused his name to be synonymous with perfidy to this day, may actually have been written with an idealistic motivation. "Machiavellianism" was a fact in Italy long before he was born; he simply studied the past and looked around him, observed the climate and applied himself to an analysis of how to thrive in it. Italy at that time, and for many years before and after, was not a nation but, as Machiavelli wrote, "more enslaved than the Hebrews, more downtrodden than the Persians, more disunited than the Athenians, without a chief, without order, beaten, despoiled, mangled, overrun, subject to every sort of desolation." It was his hope that the Italian peninsula could be united under one powerful ruler. He saw no possibility of improving human nature; his hypothetical ruler would have to accept a world in which any means, no matter how repugnant, was justified by its end, and in which success was the only criterion of behavior. In order to establish and maintain unity, the prince should abolish the *condottieri* system and rely on native militia—who could be depended upon so long as the prince governed with reasonable justice. For a time, Machiavelli saw in Cesare Borgia the man who might accomplish all this. In judging Machiavelli, 20th Century ideals of freedom and decency must be set aside, and the facts of Renaissance life substituted. The philosopher Hegel once summed it up: "The most reckless violence, all kinds of deception, murder, and the like" were then acceptable because "the despots who had to be subdued were assailable in no other way, inasmuch as indomitable lawlessness and perfect depravity were thoroughly engrained in them."

In person, Machiavelli was a gentle soul and a good friend to Leonardo. After they left Borgia's company, Machiavelli, using his position as chancellor of the Florentine government, obtained for Leonardo one of the most important commissions in his career: the *Battle of Anghiari.* The Florentines wanted to have the walls of their council chamber decorated with scenes from the city's military history, and it was arranged that both Leonardo and Michelangelo should paint them. (In passing, it is hard not to put an exclamation point after those facts. Can one imagine what a museum, a city, a government, might pay to have the two titans simultaneously at their command? It might be added that a third artist, then about 21, often visited the chamber to see the works in progress: Raphael.

The actual battle of Anghiari, in which the Florentines defeated the Milanese in 1440, was a trivial affair in which only one man was killed. However, one incident stuck deeply in Leonardo's mind: a fight, involving a few cavalrymen, that swirled around a battle standard. Leonardo's sketches for the large wallpainting indicate that he intended to include a panorama of combat, with the struggle for the standard as its centerpiece. In a phrase which must by now have become sadly monotonous, Leonardo's painting has been lost. He completed his cartoon (also lost) and actually put his colors on the wall, where they remained, slowly deteriorating, for about 60 years. As in the *Last Supper* he experimented —and the experiment was a failure with large areas of paint melting and running down the wall.

The painting was not a total ruin; several copies of it were made before it was finally given up for lost and painted over—coincidentally by Leonardo's biographer Vasari, whose second-rate mural remains on the wall today. The contemporary copies give a fair indication of Leonardo's outlines, but they were by inferior hands. It was not until about 1605 when another genius, Peter Paul Rubens, visited Italy that something approximating Leonardo's real intent was recaptured. As a great artist, Rubens understood Leonardo, and even though the drawing he made is only a copy of copies, it is generally agreed that through it one may come close to visualizing the lost work *(page 155)*.

Leonardo's central design for the *Battle* was hexagonal in shape, a tangle of men and horses so closely knit that it could well be a study for sculpture. The rearing horses are echoes of those in the early, pioneering work of Leonardo, the *Adoration of the Magi,* but the human emotion they reciprocate here is not joy but fury: while the warriors slash at each other, the animals kick and bite. The painting may be regarded as a crystallization of Leonardo's attitude toward war, which he called *pazzia bestialissima*—most beastly madness—a view which no doubt was particularly strong in his mind after his experience with Cesare Borgia. He meant it to be a terrible and timeless indictment, as valid today as in the Renaissance. There is therefore no setting, and the fantastic costumes of the warriors belong to no specific period. To make his crystallization even more striking, Leonardo caused the lines of his composition—the swords, the faces of the men, the curves of the horses' bodies and the thrust of their legs, all to radiate inward. There is nothing to lead the eye away from the center of this "indictment," which lies like some damning piece of evidence placed alone on a bare table by a prosecutor.

Leonardo and Michelanglo were not painting in competition with each other; at least the Grand Council seems to have had no intention of pitting one artist against the other. They made their cartoons in different parts of the city, at slightly different times, and there was no confrontation in the great hall. But each artist must have sensed that there was a competition in spirit if not in fact. In drawing horses, Leonardo did what he was popularly thought to do best; Michelangelo chose *his* forte, the male nude, for his cartoon of the *Battle of Cascina.* For some years the two cartoons remained in the hall (Michelangelo did not produce a finished painting either, or even begin one), constituting what Benvenuto Cellini called "the school of the world."

Soon after his commission for the *Battle* Leonardo received an honor which had an ironic twist. He was asked to serve on a committee to decide where in Florence the great marble *David,* created by Michelangelo, should be placed. Whatever his feelings, Leonardo stifled them and served, but there is in his *Comparison of the Arts* a tart section aimed at someone whose identity is not hard to surmise. "I do not find any difference between painting and sculpture except this: the sculptor pursues his work with greater physical effort, and the painter pursues his with greater mental effort. This may be proved, for the sculptor in producing his work makes a manual effort in striking the marble or stone, whichever it is, to remove what is superfluous and extends beyond the figure shut in it. This demands a wholly mechanical exercise that is often accompanied by much sweat and this combines with the dust and turns into a crust of dirt. His face is covered with this paste and powdered with marble dust, like a baker, and he is covered with tiny chips as if it had snowed on him. His lodgings are dirty and filled with stone splinters and dust.

"In the case of the painter (and we are speaking of the best among painters as among sculptors), just the opposite occurs. He sits at great ease in front of his work, well dressed, moving a light brush with agreeable colors; he is adorned with such garments as he pleases, and his dwelling is clean and filled with beautiful paintings. He often has himself accompanied with music or the sound of different, beautiful works being read, which he may hear with great pleasure, undisturbed by the pounding of hammers or other noises."

At about the time of his service on the committee, and while he was still considering his cartoon for the *Battle of Anghiari,* Leonardo began work on what was to become one of the most famous paintings on earth, the *Mona Lisa.* It is unique—and so, in literature, is Walter Pater's description of it *(page 140).* One can add nothing to Pater's description of the face. However, because he assigned himself a limited space in dealing with Leonardo in *The Renaissance,* Pater was obliged to omit some points of interest. The painting is so familiar, so deeply fixed in men's minds, that it is difficult to believe that it ever had a different appearance than it now has. Nonetheless it does not look as it did on the day it left Leonardo's hands. Once there were colonnettes on both sides, now cut away, which made plain that the lady was seated on a balcony and not, as it presently appears, somehow suspended in space. The coloring of the face, the crimson tones mentioned by Vasari, are no longer visible; darkened varnishes have changed the whole balance of colors, creating a muted, underwater effect which is made even worse by the oyster-colored light that filters weakly down on the painting from the skylight in the Grand Gallery of the Louvre. These changes, however, are merely unfortunate, not tragic; the masterpiece remains, and one must be grateful that it has survived as well as it has.

Mona Lisa was not Leonardo's ideal of beauty, as many believe—that ideal may be seen in the face of the angel in the *Madonna of the Rocks.*

Yet he must have seen in *Mona Lisa* another sort of ideal that so impressed him that he rejected other valuable commissions in order to work for perhaps three years on her portrait; and the painting *is*, on one level, a portrait of a specific human being. Mona Lisa—a contraction of Madonna Lisa—was the third wife of a Florentine merchant named Francesco di Bartolommeo del Giocondo (hence the painting's alternative name, *La Gioconda*). At the time of her first sitting for Leonardo she was about 24, or, in Renaissance terms, approaching middle age. As a portrait the work was superbly successful, in Vasari's words "an exact copy of nature." But Leonardo far transcended portraiture to make his subject not only a woman, but Woman; in his hands the individual and the symbolic became one. The artist's view of symbolic Woman may not coincide with that of most men—Leonardo regarded her with a disquieting lack of normal sensuality, so that she appears at once voluptuous and cold, beautiful and yet faintly repulsive. The painting is not large in its dimensions but impresses the viewer as monumental, an effect achieved by Leonardo's placement of the figure in relation to the background. This monumentality greatly heightens the mingled sense of charm and chill that radiates from the *Mona Lisa;* for centuries men have looked at her with delight, with puzzlement, or with something approaching dread.

In the technique of the painting Leonardo brought his use of *sfumato* to perfection—a dozen, scores, perhaps a hundred infinitely thin glazes are laid on the panel. His background, too, is perhaps his finest *(page 141).* Its details are precise, but its spires of rock and its water, the bones and blood of the earth, bring to mind a romantic vision of the earth on the day after Creation. The painting has been so often imitated and has had so much—indeed, too much—influence in art that it is difficult to take a fresh view of it, but a prolonged study of the colorplate on page 140 will bring a surprising revelation even to those who are weary of the *Mona Lisa,* or who now believe they are.

A s he worked on the *Mona Lisa* Leonardo lost interest in the *Battle of Anghiari.* The damage to the latter was such that a fresh start was required, but he had little inclination to begin again. However the Florentine Council took the businesslike view that he should repair the painting, produce another, or repay the money given him. As the pressure increased, Leonardo was happily extricated from the situation by Charles d'Amboise, Lord of Chaumont, who was governing Milan for Louis XII of France. The French had great admiration for Leonardo—Louis had been so impressed by the *Last Supper* that, upon first seeing it, he had asked his engineers if it could not somehow be removed from the wall and transported to France, even if it meant demolishing the monastery. Louis must also have admired *The Horse,* which was then still majestic despite what his bowmen had done to it, and enchanted by Leonardo's other work still in Milan. The Florentines thus received a letter from Charles d'Amboise, perhaps dictated by the King, requesting that Leonardo be sent to Milan to perform certain work. The Council was in no position to refuse a request backed by French military power, and so agreed to let him go, stipulating that he return in three months. As matters developed, it turned out to be a very long three months indeed.

A year or so after he finished the *Mona Lisa,* Leonardo was at work on *Leda and the Swan.* The finest representation of this lost work is a pen-and-ink drawing by Raphael *(detail above),* presumed to be almost a direct copy of the panel painting by Leonardo. Raphael, when he reached his artistic maturity only a few years after making this copy, used the stance of the Leda figure for one of his philosophers in his Vatican fresco *School of Athens.*

The Science of Art

No great artist has ever addressed his fellow professionals with so remarkable a discourse on technique as Leonardo did in his *Treatise on Painting*. Although works such as the *Mona Lisa* contain passages far too deep and imaginative to be prescribed in a textbook, he believed that painting is governed by laws and principles which lend themselves to codification almost as well as those of mathematics. In a random sampling of his precepts one finds: "When you have to draw from nature, stand three times as far away as the size of the object that you are drawing. . . . Every opaque object that is devoid of color partakes of the color of that which is opposite to it, as happens with a white wall. . . . The shadows cast by trees on which the sun is shining are as dark as that of the center of the tree. . . . The sun will appear greater in moving water or when the surface is broken into waves than it does in still water."

On the following pages are examples of Leonardo's application of his precepts to his work and of the evolution of his thought concerning such themes as the *Adoration of the Magi (opposite)* and the *Virgin and Child with St. Anne*. That he practiced what he preached is plain; so, too, is his opinion about the role of the intellect in artistic creation. "Those who are enamored of practice without science," he wrote, "are like a pilot who goes into a ship without rudder or compass and never has any certainty where he is going."

Leonardo's study for the *Adoration of the Magi* follows his teachings: "Let the sketches for historical subjects be rapid, and the working of the limbs not too much finished. Content yourself with merely giving the positions of these limbs, which you will then be able at your leisure to finish as you please."

Composition sketch for
Adoration of the Magi, c. 1481

"How the Ages of Man Should Be Depicted"

Although Leonardo's plans for illustrating his *Treatise on Painting* are unknown, quotations from it can be matched with drawings, as at left: "Old men should be shown with slow, listless movements, with the legs bent at the knees when they are standing up, with the feet parallel and separated one from another, the spine bent low, the head leaning forward, and the arms not too far apart."

Studies of single figures, c. 1481

In his studies for an Adoration, Leonardo's drawing precisely follows his instructions: "Women should be represented in modest attitudes, with legs close together, arms folded, and with their heads low and bending sideways. . . . Little children should be represented when sitting as twisting themselves about with quick movements, and in shy, timid attitudes when standing up."

Studies of a Virgin adoring the Infant Christ, c. 1483

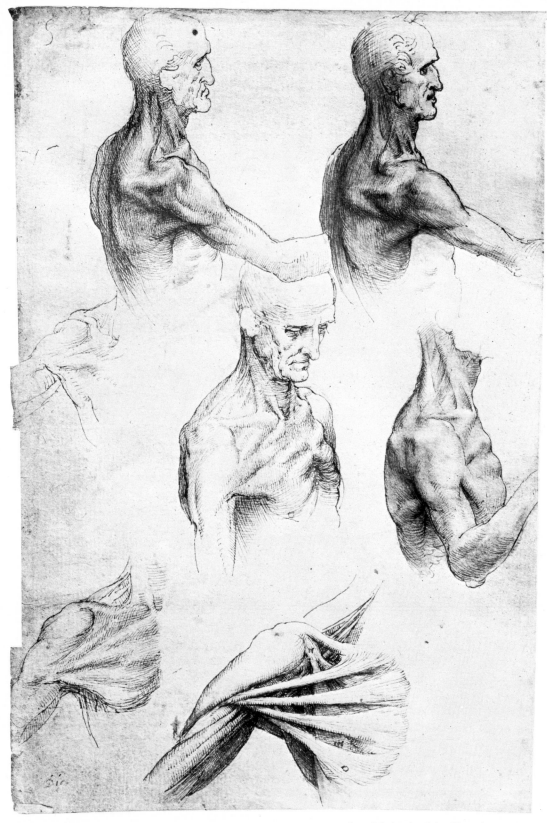

Studies of the head and shoulders of a man, 1510

"How It Is Necessary To Know the Inner Structure of Man"

"The painter who has acquired a knowledge of the nature of the sinews, muscles and tendons," Leonardo wrote, "will know exactly in the movement of any limb how many and which of the sinews are the cause of it, and which muscle by its swelling is the cause of this sinew's contracting." He often studied lean, living men.

The exquisite little drawing of a tree at left was probably made by Leonardo to illustrate his *Treatise.* The commentary reads: "The part of a tree which has shadow for background is all of one tone, and wherever the trees or branches are thickest they will be darkest. . . . But where the boughs lie against a background of other boughs, the brighter parts are seen lightest and the leaves lustrous from the sunlight."

In the red-chalk study on the opposite page Leonardo shows masterfully how a rainstorm should be drawn. The scene is an Alpine valley plunged into shadows by the advance of massed clouds discharging torrents of water; the slanting lines of rain, done with quick strokes of the chalk, veil the background like gauze. The drawing, made about 1499, is among the last of his naturalistic treatments of landscape.

The mountains *(below),* doubtless drawn in the Italian Alps, illustrate Leonardo's discussion of atmospheric depth: that air nearest the ground is dense, while "the higher it rises the lighter and more transparent it becomes. . . . Therefore, O painter, when you represent mountains, see that . . . the bases are always paler than the summits . . . and the loftier they are the more they should reveal their true shape and color."

Study of a tree, c. 1498

Study of mountain ranges, 1511

A Storm over an Alpine Valley, c. 1499

133

Perspective study for the background of the *Adoration of the Magi*, c. 1481

As Leonardo developed his ideas for the *Adoration of the Magi* from
such hastily drawn sketches as that shown on page 129, he made a
study for the background *(above)*, which is a perfect illustration of
mathematical, linear perspective. There all lines converge on a
vanishing point at right center. From this firm scientific base his
imagination, expressed in the swarming figures, leaped up into a
world of mystery, so that this extraordinary drawing transcends
its original purpose and sums up the quality of his mind.

Working on the painting of the *Adoration* itself, Leonardo changed
his conception still further. The drawings, for example, had
contained vestiges of the roof of the stable in which Christ was
born—here they disappear. Although he completed only the
underpainting in oil on the panel, his chiaroscuro even at this
stage produced a three-dimensional roundness in the figures,
which is readily apparent at right and even more markedly so in
the enlarged detail shown on the following pages.

Adoration of the Magi, 1481–1482

Burlington House Cartoon, c. 1499

Two works, one produced near the beginning and one at the end of Leonardo's preoccupation with the theme of the Virgin and Child with St. Anne, show the intellectual labor he put into composition. The early version above (called the *Burlington House Cartoon* after the British collection which once owned it) is essentially vertical and classical: a composition of Grecian beauty. But as Clark writes: ". . . . The classical elements in his work, like the geometrical, are a result of study, not predisposition." Some 10 years later, in the unfinished Louvre painting, Leonardo had changed his composition to a pyramid, with complex curving lines which fully express his own instinctive style.

Virgin and Child with St. Anne, 1500-1510

Mona Lisa, 1503

In no other of Leonardo's paintings are the depths and haze of atmosphere more fully re-created than in the background *(right)* of the *Mona Lisa.* This is aerial perspective at its finest. Yet it is the face that forever holds the eye, and has caused the work to be more often copied than any other—"this beauty, into which the soul with all its maladies has passed!" wrote Walter Pater. "All the thoughts and experience of the world have etched and moulded there . . . the animalism of Greece, the lust of Rome, the mysticism of the middle age . . . the return of the Pagan world, the sins of the Borgias. She is older than the rocks among which she sits; like the vampire, she has been dead many times, and learned the secrets of the grave; and has been a diver in deep seas . . . and trafficked for strange webs with Eastern merchants, and, as Leda, was the mother of Helen of Troy, and, as Saint Anne, the mother of Mary; and all this has been to her but as the sound of lyres and flutes."

Mona Lisa, detail

The most controversial version of the *Mona Lisa* is in the Vernon collection in the U.S. Its owners consider it authentic and value it at $2.5 million.

This copy in The Walters Art Gallery, Baltimore, like the Vernon version, shows the flanking colonnettes that were later cut from the original.

This version which hangs in the Chamber of Deputies in Rome has been attributed to one of Leonardo's pupils, Bernardino Luini.

The National Gallery in Oslo owns this copy, signed "Bernardino Luini. MDXXV" but possibly painted by Philippe de Champaigne.

The *Mona Lisa* in the Prado, Madrid, is the work of an unknown 16th Century artist who chose to omit Leonardo's background.

A copy in the collection of Dr. Carl Muller, of Thalwil, Switzerland, was painted by Leonardo's untalented pupil and companion Salai.

"La Belle Gabrielle," a nude version, probably of the 16th Century, is in the collection of the Earl of Spencer at Northampton, England.

A 17th Century nude version is in the Carrara Academy in Bergamo. The *Mona Lisa* has also been copied in sculpture and often caricatured.

VII

The City
of Disillusion

Leonardo's silverpoint study for
the angel's head in the Louvre
Madonna of the Rocks (page 50) is
deceptively simple. A rain of parallel
hatchings slanting from left to
right produces a sense of depth and
plasticity, of rounded grace
emerging from a flat page,
that few artists have ever matched.

Study for the angel's head in the
Louvre *Madonna of the Rocks*, c. 1483

When the 54-year-old Leonardo was summoned to Milan in 1506 by Charles d'Amboise, the French Viceroy, there was no mention of specific tasks that d'Amboise or Louis XII wished him to undertake. Both men held him in high regard; perhaps they simply desired his presence as an ornament to the Milanese court. At any rate they had little intention of sending him back to Florence at the end of the three-month period stipulated by the Florentine Council. When the Council demanded his return so that he could fulfill his obligations regarding the *Battle of Anghiari,* Louis himself let them know how matters stood. In his capital beyond the Alps, where he was preparing for another foray into Italy, he summoned the Florentine Ambassador and gave him some rather plain instructions. "Write to the Council," said Louis, "that I desire to make use of the services of Maestro Leonardo . . . as I wish to have some works of his; and see to it that the Council authorizes him to enter my service at once, and to remain in Milan until I arrive there. And write to Florence in such a way that it will have effect, and do it at once, and let me see the letter." The unhappy Ambassador did as he was told; thereafter Leonardo was free of his obligations, and later could even visit Florence at will, with no trouble from the Council.

The French permitted Leonardo great latitude in his activities, paid him well, and apparently never made any imperious requests of him. With the exception of occasional excursions he passed the next six years in Milan, becoming ever more deeply involved in his scientific studies. The French King vaguely suggested that he would like Leonardo to produce "certain small pictures of Our Lady and others as the mood takes me, and perhaps I shall also set him to paint my portrait," but if Leonardo undertook such projects the results have long since vanished. On one occasion he journeyed northward to the Alps and climbed Monte Rosa, where he made notes on the quality of light among the snowfields and glaciers. At times he worked on the canalization of the Lombardy plain— several of his finest drawings of locks, weirs and the motion of water date from this period—and at times he resumed painting, although with increasing reliance on pupils to execute his designs. During the years

1506 to 1508, he produced the second or London version of the *Madonna of the Rocks*, which may be seen on page 51, opposite the earlier Louvre painting of the same subject.

Why Leonardo should have made two versions of this *Madonna* is a question not yet resolved. It is generally believed that the first was done to fulfill a contract signed in 1483 with the Milanese Confraternity of the Immaculate Conception. For some reason the painting was not kept by the Confraternity; eventually it passed into the hands of the French. In any case the Confraternity commissioned a second version in which Ambrogio da Predis, the Milanese artist with whom Leonardo worked during his early, impoverished days in the city, was to have a share. But unaccountably, Leonardo and da Predis did not keep their bargain; arguments and lawsuits flourished, and nearly 25 years passed before the Confraternity finally got its painting.

A comparison of the Louvre *Madonna of the Rocks* and the much later version, now in the British National Gallery, reveals the great difference between Leonardo's Quattrocento and High Renaissance styles. Although the paintings are approximately equal in size, the figures in the later version seem larger, having been brought closer to the viewer and made weightier and more ideal. The colors have been subdued, giving the figures what appears at first glance to be a corpselike pallor. Indeed, when the painting was cleaned soon after World War II, some critics found the colors so muted that they accused the National Gallery of having ruined the surface. But in fact the cleaned painting is much as Leonardo intended it to be; the colors are deliberately de-emphasized, no longer decorative but used to carry out his ideal of three-dimensional roundness. The painting reflects the long-thought-out theoretical aspects of his art, his studies of light and shade and the means of making figures appear "plastic." As a result it is not as appealing to the eye as the earlier version, but more a challenge to the mind.

The compositional changes in the second painting were apparently made to please the Confraternity—the Milanese brothers may have found the pointing gesture of the Louvre angel too cryptic and asked for its deletion. They might not have been familiar with the Florentine conception of St. John as an infant, and thus requested that he be identified by his reedy, elongated cross. It is likely that they also asked for the inclusion of halos, which otherwise appear only in Leonardo's earliest work. For his own purposes Leonardo made new studies for the angel's head, body and drapery, and the corresponding painted passages are unmistakably his. However, after he had executed the parts of most concern to him, he left much of the work to pupils and perhaps to his cocontractor, da Predis.

In the winter and spring of 1507 and 1508 Leonardo spent six months in Florence on an unpleasant personal errand. He had never been on cordial terms with his much younger half-brothers; in 1504, when his father died intestate, they had joined to deprive him of a share of the estate. In 1507 Leonardo's uncle Francesco also died, but left a will in which he remembered his brilliant nephew. The half-brothers attempted to break the will, and at that Leonardo became furious and fought them in court. Some indication of the feeling between the artist and his plodding kin may be found in a letter he wrote to one of them. It is a crystal of gall, but it was written at a time when Leonardo, growing old, had seen a great deal of this wolfish world. "My most beloved brother: This is sent merely to inform you that a short time ago I received a letter from you from which I learned that you have had an heir, which circumstance I understand has afforded you a great deal of pleasure. Now insofar as I had judged you to be possessed of prudence I am now entirely convinced that I am as far removed from having an accurate judgment as you are from prudence, seeing that you have been congratulating yourself in having created a watchful enemy who will strive with all his energies after liberty, which can only come into being at your death."

While he was in Florence engaged in his legal battle (which he won) Leonardo shared a house with the talented, eccentric young sculptor Gian Francesco Rustici. Instead of a dog, cat or even an ermine, Rustici kept a porcupine which had the run of the house; it amused him when his guests, stabbed under the table, yelped in pain. At Rustici's dinners the food, though excellent, was molded into macabre or disgusting shapes. Leonardo felt at home in this ménage, and passed much time trying to organize the mass of notes and drawings he had accumulated. For years the enormousness of this task had pressed down on him with increasing weight, and now he wrote the pathetic note containing the phrase, "Therefore, O reader, blame me not." But his melancholy moods were brief; he took delight in Rustici's company, and according to Vasari greatly helped him in making the famous group of bronze figures, *St. John, Pharisee and Levite,* which stands above the north door of the Baptistery in Florence. "While Gian Francesco was at work on the clay model for this group," Vasari wrote, "he wished no one to come near him but Leonardo da Vinci who . . . right up to the casting of the statues, never left him." The casting was actually done at some time after Leonardo left Rustici, but in other regards Vasari seems to have been right. Parts of the sculpture are Leonardesque in the extreme—it is believed by some critics that Leonardo did the actual modeling, but there is no proof of that.

Both the pose of this bronze figure of St. John and gesture of the upraised finger mark it as influenced by Leonardo's work. In fact, Gian Francesco Rustici, the sculptor, owes an even greater debt to the older master; Leonardo advised and perhaps even assisted in the casting of the work, one of a group of three executed by Rustici for the north doors of the Baptistery of the cathedral in Florence.

Aside from the Rustici group, which at most can be called a collaboration, no sculpture by Leonardo is known to exist. Despite his disparaging remarks about stone-carvers and his view that sculpture ranked below painting as an art, it is certain that *The Horse* was not his only venture into that field. A few of his drawings, showing heads and shoulders cut off cleanly by horizontal lines, are plainly studies for busts. In the Museum of Budapest there is a small equestrian statue attributed to Leonardo by a few scholars—the horse seems to have his manner, and resembles some of his sketches for the *Battle of Anghiari.* There is a drawing of horses at Windsor beside which he wrote "make a little one of wax about four inches long." However, the Budapest bronze, about nine inches in height, is probably the work of a pupil who had obtained one of Leonardo's figurines and attempted a larger copy.

The subject of Leonardo's pupils is an intriguing one. In Milan he had many, among them Giovanni Antonio Boltraffio, Marco d'Oggiono, Cesare da Sesto, Francesco Melzi and the Spaniard Fernando de Llanos. They were all studious and prolific, following Leonardo's ideas and motifs with unquestioning devotion, but none became an artist of stature. This was not because Leonardo lacked interest in teaching—his *Treatise on Painting,* though never set in order during his lifetime, is a great textbook which has been studied with reverence and profit by artists in every century since his death. But among his immediate followers he never found any who were remotely capable of absorbing all he had to teach, and he must have overawed even the best of them. In their hands Leonardo's subtle techniques became overlabored and obvious; his mysteries and ambiguities turned into lumpish statements. On their unfortunate efforts may be blamed many of the later misconceptions of Leonardo's style, since it is only through their copies that several of his major compositions are known today.

Of the young students who attached themselves to Leonardo, only one—Francesco Melzi—merits more than passing mention; and even Melzi is to be remembered not for his art, which was mediocre, but for his personal relationship to Leonardo. Melzi became his apprentice in Milan around 1507 when he was 14. Sensitive, intelligent, he soon recognized the loneliness that lay behind Leonardo's cool reserve, and to the aging and increasingly disillusioned master he became in effect a son. Unlike Salai, Melzi was neither gauche nor greedy; he came from a noble family, and although he was unable to approach Leonardo on intellectual or artistic grounds he gave him deep, protective affection, did his best to ease the discomforts of his last years, and remained with him until he died. Of all Leonardo's personal relationships, that with Melzi seems alone to have been touched with love. As he sensed the approach of death Leonardo made a will in which, at least by implication, he made peace with his half-brothers: he left them his money. But to Melzi he left all his papers and drawings. Melzi's subsequent management of this treasure may have been unwise, even tragic, but that is a matter for later consideration.

By 1508 Leonardo's career as a painter was drawing to a close, although he had more than 10 years still to live. Only two paintings survive from those years; one is the Louvre's *Virgin and Child with St. Anne,* studies for which may be dated as early as 1500, though the painting was still in progress in 1510—probably he worked intermittently on it throughout the period and abandoned it, unfinished, in the latter year. Though it is incomplete, it is Leonardo's final statement of the theme that had intrigued him for a very long time, and of which the earliest surviving version is the *Burlington House Cartoon.* In contrast with the perfect balance and verticality of the *Cartoon,* the painting is filled with twisting, diagonal motion. Within a basically pyramidal form, the curving lines of limbs and bodies lock and interlock, echo and re-echo. In his preoccupation with the design of curves, Leonardo deliberately distorted the figures —the seating of Mary on the lap of St. Anne, which seems a natural and unobtrusive arrangement in the *Cartoon,* strikes some observers as ungraceful in the painting. However that may be, one soon forgets it in studying the wonderful dynamics of the work. Against the foil of St.

Anne's maternal quietness, Mary's almost acrobatic pose is deeply arresting as she bends sharply forward to restrain her Son. Leonardo, compounding centuries of religious dogma with the subtlest understanding of human emotion, indicates the indecision of the mother of Jesus as she tries to hold Him back from His destiny, the Passion in the form of the sacrificial lamb which He, smiling, tries to seize. The surfaces of Mary's face and her outer garment are unfinished, but the background is complete in detail; with its delicate tones of gray and faint blue, it suggests a craggy, silent world or moon on which neither life nor death exists.

Leonardo's final engagement with sculpture—brilliant in concept, immensely powerful even in the sketches that remain, although no part of it was ever cast or carved—dates from about 1511, as he neared the age of 60. At that time Gian Giacomo Trivulzio, a Milanese *condottiere* who had taken service with the French, requested him to make a tomb memorial, an equestrian statue on an elaborate base in which Trivulzio's body was eventually to be placed. Nearly 30 years after his studies for Sforza's *Horse* Leonardo considered again the possibilities of a prancing animal, and although he still had his earlier drawings at hand, set out with characteristic thoroughness to make an entirely new series. His ideal of perfection had greatly advanced; he no longer thought of horse and rider as separate units to be made individually and later joined, but as a dynamic whole. The lines of his Trivulzio studies, mostly done in ink and the black chalk that he adopted late in his career, show a sculpturesque emphasis on weight and volume; the shading is no longer in diagonal left-to-right strokes, but follows the natural contours of his subject, and in the case of chalk is rubbed and modeled with the fingers. His design for the pedestal is full of classical detail—columns, frieze, cornice and architrave—but so transmuted by Leonardo that it was, or would have been, a masterwork of the High Renaissance.

That the Trivulzio monument never advanced beyond the stage of drawing cannot be fairly blamed on Leonardo. In 1512 an alliance of Swiss, Spaniards, Venetians and papal forces drove the French out of Milan —a relatively minor setback for them, in the eyes of history, but for Leonardo an absolute disaster. At 60, when he might have expected to spend his final years in the comfort and honor accorded him by understanding men, he suddenly found himself without patronage or income, in a position verging on that of a suppliant. His fame, once great, had faded, and he had behind him a series of public and private failures that might have prompted a lesser man to consider suicide. And although he had never expressed a need for companionship, certainly Leonardo must have glanced around him at this time and seen only the faithful, warmhearted but very young Francesco Melzi, and the leechlike Salai.

The new rulers of Milan were not actively hostile to Leonardo—they ignored him. Apparently he spent several months in 1513 at the villa of the Melzi family in nearby Vaprio d'Adda considering what alternatives were left to him, and in February of that year fate provided what seemed a likely one. Pope Julius II died and was succeeded by Leo X—a Medici. To be sure, the Medici had shown Leonardo no special favor in Florence, but they were patrons of art, and it apparently occurred to

These sketches for the Trivulzio monument, the last sculptural project Leonardo undertook, show significant changes from his designs for the colossal horse commissioned 20 years earlier by Lodovico Sforza. Horse and rider are conceived as one; the monument as a whole would have been a free-standing architectural structure, with columns supporting the life-sized equestrian statue and space for a sarcophagus below.

Leonardo that they might now help him. In September 1513, the tiring but courageous old man set out for Rome.

On his journey southward Leonardo was full of high spirits, if Vasari's account is correct: "On the way he made a paste with wax and constructed hollow animals which flew in the air when blown up, but fell when the wind ceased." In Rome he was welcomed, as he had hoped, by Giuliano de' Medici, the Pope's kindly though weak and bumbling brother, and given rooms in the Belvedere Palace of the Vatican, together with a small allowance. Vasari continues: "On a curious lizard found by the vine-dresser of the Belvedere he fastened scales taken from other lizards, dipped in quicksilver, which trembled as it moved, and after giving it eyes, a horn and a beard, he tamed it and kept it in a box. All the friends to whom he showed it ran away terrified."

The story of the lizard toy is entirely credible, particularly as one recalls Leonardo's first venture into art in the painting of the peasant's shield many years before. But the phrase "all the friends" has an unintentionally ironic sound. What friends? The lions of Rome were the old architect Bramante, whom Leonardo had known well in Milan; Michelangelo; and in particular Raphael, the young man who owed such a great artistic debt to Leonardo. So far as is known, none paid any attention to Leonardo. He was passé. Raphael, the Pope's favorite, received thousands of ducats for his work in the Vatican; Leonardo was obliged to live on 33 a month. The voracious Isabella d'Este, who for years had used all her wiles to extract a painting from Leonardo, came to Rome to besiege the "important" artist of the day—Raphael. It is doubtful that she bothered to get in touch with Leonardo.

At one time Pope Leo X was persuaded to give Leonardo a small commission—subject unknown—but the result was disastrous. Leonardo, absorbed as always in technical matters, commenced to compound a special varnish for the unpainted picture. The Pope threw up his hands, crying, "This man will never accomplish anything! He thinks of the end before the beginning." There were no further papal assignments. At about this time Leonardo made an entry in one of his notebooks, written in an extremely small hand as though he were whispering to himself: "We should not desire the impossible." His notes also began to be sprinkled with a constantly repeated, melancholy question: "Tell me if anything was ever done. . . . Was anything ever done. . . . Tell me if. . . ."

He fell ill. In his Roman papers there is the address of a physician, not in Leonardo's handwriting. The nature of the illness is unknown, but it may well have been a minor stroke, the forerunner of others that later paralyzed his right hand and eventually killed him. However, he soon recovered and pressed on with his scientific inquiries, studying the immense variety of plants in the Pope's botanical garden and dissecting cadavers in the Roman hospital. He made plans for draining the Pontine marshes and notes for a treatise on the mechanics of the human voice, with which he hoped to regain the favor of the Pope. Leonardo gave the treatise to some bored papal official; he did not hear of it again.

Leonardo's sole self-portrait was apparently made during his stay in Rome when he was about 62. Done in red chalk, it reveals a massive, furrowed forehead, piercing but sad, pained eyes, a downturned mouth and a cascade of beard. It is said that Leonardo, despite his physical strength, came prematurely to old age, and here is the proof of it. The face seems that of an ancient, disillusioned prophet.

Leonardo's last painting was also completed in Rome, evidently without commission from anyone; a work that some inner compulsion obliged him to produce. It is the Louvre's *St. John,* by far the most disquieting of all his pictures, and one that many of his admirers wish he had never made. In Leonardo's vision, the ascetic precursor of Christ, whom one imagines to have been a gaunt firebrand of a man, becomes almost hermaphrodite. Soft-fleshed, his womanish arm bent across his breast, he glances out of the painting with a look that expresses not annunciation but mystery. Leonardo's two characteristic devices, the gentle, baffling smile and the upraised forefinger pointing heavenward, are so dominant in the *St. John* that they are only a hairbreadth from self-satire.

It may have been Leonardo's intention, in the last painting of his life, to state his hard-won view that all that can be learned of the flesh, the world and the universe can be summed up in the curve of a question mark. However, although he was finished with painting, he was not yet finished with the world. He now destroyed it. In 10 black-chalk drawings collectively known as *The Deluge,* together with awesome written description in his notebooks, he pictured the end of creation with tremendous power and—it cannot be denied—with something akin to relish.

The idea of apocalyptic destruction had long been in Leonardo's mind. But when he turned in earnest to his dreadful theme he departed entirely from traditional ideas and drew on his own scientific investigations and beliefs: the earth and the mountains had been molded by the forces of tempest and flood; the same forces would destroy all.

In drawing the beginning of the Deluge, Leonardo sketched gigantic torrents descending from the raging sky, sweeping the whole landscape before them. In the Deluge at its height, Leonardo abandoned all classical tradition; his drawings are almost nonobjective in their power of pure design. Nothing remains but elemental force; no man, no earth, no God.

The sledge-hammering violence of the Deluge drawings reminds one of nothing so much as the ending of a Beethoven symphony. It would seem that only silence is to follow; that Leonardo will cease his questioning—"Tell me, tell me if anything was ever done." But it was not yet time for him to die. Often in music, after the seemingly final thunder, there is a gentle little coda. And so in Leonardo's case there was. Overshadowed though he may have been in Rome, the French had not forgotten him. Louis XII had died, but a deep respect for Leonardo remained in Louis' successor, Francis I. Young King Francis offered Leonardo a manor house in France, not far from the royal chateau in Amboise, together with whatever funds the old man might require. In return, Francis wished only the pleasure of Leonardo's conversation. Accordingly he went northward into an alien land, taking with him what must have been the most wondrous cargo in the history of art: his notes, his drawings, the *St. John,* the *Virgin and Child with St. Anne* and a portrait described as "of a certain Florentine lady."

"Earth... to Heaven"

In his prodigious creation of drawings Leonardo used every technique then known and is believed to have developed still others. Some he drew in fine sharpened red chalk; he was, if not the originator, surely the first master of this technique. He has been credited with the invention of pastel; although it is not found in his own work, it first appears in that of his pupils. His silverpoint drawings are done on the widest range of colored backgrounds, from pale green to pinkish buff, blue, purple and orange, and invariably with an exquisite touch.

Few masters have approached Leonardo's ability to create three-dimensional effects by graphic means. A glance at some of the rapid preliminary studies on following pages shows how, by the mere swelling of a line, the torsions and curves of the body are expressed. His favorite medium was pen and ink, which enabled him to turn without interruption from illustration to the written commentary which so often supplemented his work. The most acute comment ever made upon Leonardo's drawing comes from the great Renaissance authority Bernard Berenson: "The quality of qualities, then, in Leonardo's drawing is the feeling it gives of unimpeded, untroubled, unaltered transfer of the object in his vision to the paper. . . . And yet so little of effort is there to be perceived in this wonderful alchemy, that it is as if suddenly, by the mere feat of a demiurge, earth were transubstantiated to Heaven."

Leonardo's study for the head of the *Litta Madonna,* drawn with a thin silver stylus on greenish prepared paper, combines compassion and resignation in overwhelming unity. The completed painting, heavily reworked or perhaps executed by another hand, appears on page 185.

Study for the head of the *Litta Madonna,* c. 1480

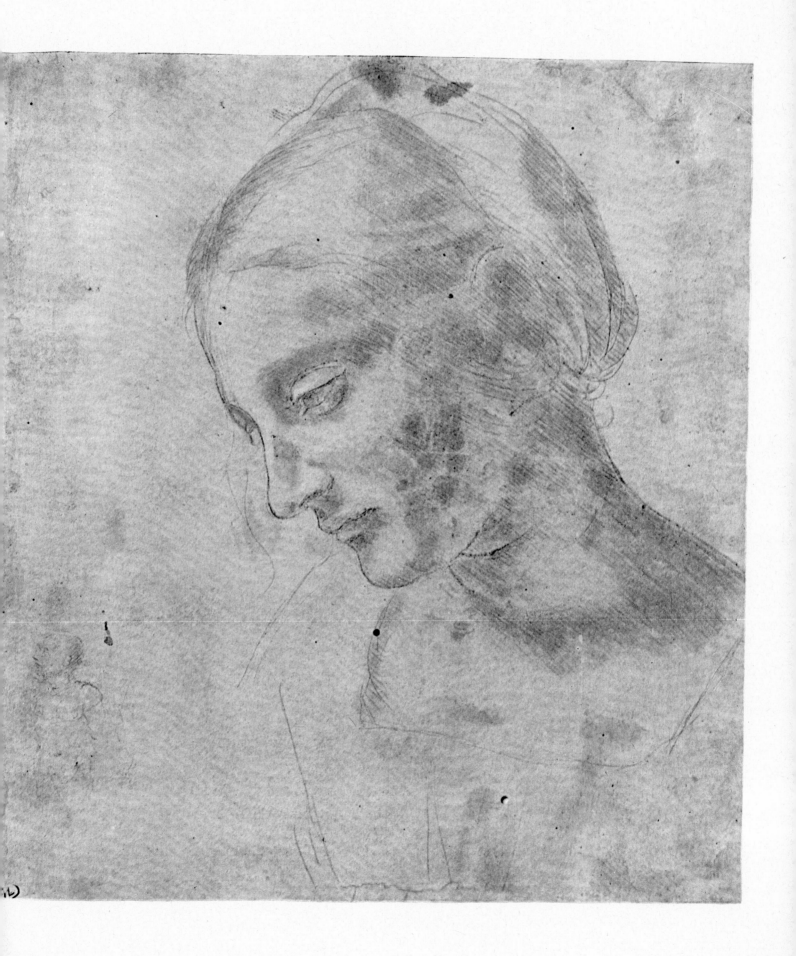

153

Head of a man shouting and a profile; study for the *Battle of Anghiari*, c. 1503

Leonardo's black- and red-chalk studies for heads in the *Battle of Anghiari* are perfect visual realizations of what he called *pazzia bestialissima* (most beastly madness). Above, the larger, screaming face at first seems dominant —until one sees, in the smaller, with what awesome skill Leonardo has drawn the grim ambivalence of love and death. At right, his forehead savagely low beneath the suggestion of helmet, a young man shouts in unreasoning wrath. Here the medium of red chalk allowed Leonardo to expand his plastic range: he turned the chalk on its side, manipulating it and rubbing it with his fingers. Above, right, is Peter Paul Rubens' drawing after the central portion of Leonardo's lost battle scene.

Peter Paul Rubens, after Leonardo:
Fight for the Standard, c. 1605

Profile of a man shouting; study for the *Battle of Anghiari*, c. 1503

Study for the *Madonna of the Yarn Winder*, probably 150

Neptune with Four Sea-Horses, c. 1503

Of the creations of Leonardo's greatest period of productivity—from 1503 to 1508 in Florence—suggestions of many remain only in his sketches and cartoons. He completed a painting known as the *Madonna of the Yarn Winder;* the winder, shaped like a cross, symbolized the Passion toward which the infant Christ eagerly stretched His arms. For this work, perhaps the finest study is a red-chalk drawing *(left)* of the Virgin's shoulders in which firmness and grace are incomparably combined. Leonardo also designed, for his classically inclined friend Antonio Segni, a fountain of Neptune; a preliminary drawing *(above)* survives. In a critical note, he reminded himself to "lower the horses," so that the sea god might appear loftier and more august.

157

Madonna and Child with a Plate of Fruit, c. 1478

Madonna and Child with a Cat, recto, probably 1478

Madonna and Child with a Cat, verso, probably 1478

The drawings reproduced here date from the 1470s, when Leonardo was in his twenties, and at first glance may appear of less interest than the more finished silverpoints and red-chalk studies on the preceding pages. However, this is in no sense true; Leonardo was engrossed not in producing detailed studies but in establishing compositions. His sketch, the *Madonna and Child with a Plate of Fruit (left)*, for all its abbreviations and economy of line, is one of the most arresting of his drawings. The rhythmic relation between the two heads, as one critic points out, "is as spontaneous and as inevitable as the relation between two bars of Mozart."

Above, Leonardo experiments with two versions of the Madonna and Child, one the reverse of the other, having been traced through the back of the paper. Both are in ink superimposed on sketches made with a stylus, although at the left he also uses wash. The little drawing at right, *Maiden with a Unicorn,* the symbol of chastity, may well have been executed for some Florentine festival allegory.

Maiden with a Unicorn, c. 1478

159

Study for *Leda and the Swan*, c. 1504

Late in his career Leonardo turned to classical mythology, to which he had previously paid scant heed, for the subject of a lost painting, *Leda and the Swan*. Several of his black-chalk sketches, reinforced with ink, survive; two are of particular interest. On the right-hand page his characteristic left-to-right strokes are supplemented by curved hatching that emphasizes Leda's turning motion. Below, her entire figure is modeled in these curving lines, creating a sense of writing that suggests fertility. The change in style, which became an obvious characteristic as Leonardo neared his fifties, indicates the continuing vitality of his mind and his willingness to think in new or different terms. The signature is not his, having been added by some later owner of the drawing.

Study for *Leda and the Swan*, c. 1504

Studies of a woman's head and coiffure, for *Leda and the Swan*, c. 1506

VIII

The Myth
and the Man

Francis I was not the greatest intellectual ever to occupy the throne of France; his predilections were for women, jousting, pageantry and fine ornament. However, even though he may not have fully understood the rare old find he had imported from Italy, he had an appreciation of genius and the humility to honor it. When Leonardo arrived in 1516 or 1517 at the royal castle at Amboise, some 100 miles southwest of Paris on the River Loire, he was given the title of *"Premier peinctre et ingenieur et architecte du Roy"*—not because of anything he was expected to do but because of what he had already done. Francis assigned him quarters in the comfortable manor house of Cloux half a mile down a winding road from the castle and frequently visited him there, taking the considerate view that it was easier for a vigorous 22-year-old King to call on an infirm 64-year-old artist than vice versa.

The indelible impression that Leonardo made on his host was noted by Benvenuto Cellini, who followed Leonardo into French service 24 years later and wrote in his *Memoirs* that "King Francis being violently enamored of his great talents took so great a pleasure in hearing him discourse that there were few days in the year when he was separated from him. . . . He said that he did not believe that there had ever been another man born into the world who had known as much as Leonardo, and this not only in matters concerning Sculpture, Painting and Architecture, but because he was a great Philosopher."

In 1517 Cardinal Louis of Aragon visited Leonardo in his manor; a record of the visit was made by the Cardinal's secretary, Antonio de Beatis. "On the 10th of October, 1517, Monsignor and the rest of us went to see, in one of the outlying parts of Amboise, Messer Lunardo Vinci the Florentine, an old graybeard of more than 70 years, the most excellent painter of our time, who showed His Excellency three pictures, one of a certain Florentine lady done from the life at the instance of the late Magnificent, Giuliano de' Medici, another of St. John the Baptist as a youth, and one of the Madonna and Child in the lap of St. Anne, all most perfect, and from whom, since he was then subject to a certain paralysis of the right hand, one could not expect any more good work." The note

A hurricane of wind and water driving upon a valley launches Leonardo's epic studies of *Apocalyptic Visions*. Almost like the storm itself, his pen and ink lines, swirling over a black-chalk base, explode on the page in a masterful demonstration of controlled despair.

Apocalyptic Visions (Last Judgment), c. 1511-1512

then describes "an infinite number of volumes all in the vulgar tongue" concerning anatomy, hydraulics, machinery and other matters, "which if they should be published will be profitable and very enjoyable."

The Cardinal's secretary was judging by appearance—at the time of the visit Leonardo was 65, not in his seventies, although doubtless he seemed ancient. It is likely that his right hand, perhaps even his arm, had indeed been paralyzed by a stroke; but apparently the secretary did not observe that Leonardo was left-handed and hence still quite capable of producing further work, as evidenced by later manuscript entries in a firm, clear script. Of the three paintings mentioned, the St. John and the St. Anne are readily identifiable. The "certain Florentine lady," in the opinion of most scholars, was the *Mona Lisa*. Possibly it was another portrait of which no record and no copies exist—Giuliano de' Medici surely had nothing to do with the *Mona Lisa*—but the probability is that the secretary, overwhelmed as he must have been at the time, inadvertently dropped the Medici name in the wrong place.

Leonardo, despite his illness and the cordial attentions of King Francis, who was prone to come jangling into the manor at all hours with some such proposition as "Tell me about the soul," did manage a little work at Amboise. Almost certainly he did no painting, except perhaps to add a touch or two to the works still in his possession. He was interested in the canalization of the Loire and its tributaries; two hydrographic studies, bearing the names of French rivers, survive. Apparently he drew plans and perhaps even supervised the laying of foundations (which have only recently been excavated) for a vast castle-town project Francis intended to construct at Romorantin. He seems also to have been involved in the staging of royal pageants—the last of his costume drawings are believed to date from about 1512, shortly before he left Milan for Rome, but conceivably a few may have been made in France as late as 1517 or 1518. In contemporary records of a pageant held at the nearby castle of Blois there is an account of a mechanical lion that few if any men save Leonardo would have had the whim and the ingenuity to construct. The large toy animal, possibly moved by springs, is said to have taken several steps toward the King as though to attack him. When the King struck the lion with a wand it stopped, opened its breast, and revealed a cluster of white French lilies on a blue field.

Of Leonardo's other activities in France very little is known. One can imagine him, like some aged Prospero, sinking peacefully into dreams and death. Among his last drawings there is one, perhaps a self-portrait in spirit although not in fact, which shows an old man seated on a riverbank, sunk in meditation so deep that it appears that only the last trumpet can rouse him. He died on May 2, 1519, a year after making the will in which he left all his drawings and papers to Francesco Melzi, some money to his half-brothers, and a vineyard near Milan to Salai.

As soon as Leonardo was in his grave, the mists that had enshrouded him in his life began to deepen; they became clouds upon which he was borne upward in a process of apotheosis. Only 31 years after his death, Vasari introduced Leonardo to posterity thus: "The richest gifts are occasionally seen to be showered, as by celestial influence, on certain human beings, nay, they sometimes supernaturally and marvelously congregate in one sole person; beauty, grace and talent being united in such a manner that to whatever the man thus favored turns himself, his every action is so divine as to leave all other men behind him, and manifestly to prove that he has been specially endowed by the hand of God Himself." Scrupulous though Vasari attempted to be in his biography of Leonardo, he nonetheless wrote a death scene for the artist which is plainly tendentious, befitting the "divine" being he had previously established. "He was then seized with a paroxysm, the harbinger of death, so that the King rose and took his head to assist him and show him favor as well as to alleviate the pain. Leonardo's divine spirit, then recognizing that he could not enjoy a greater honor, expired in the King's arms."

Actually, King Francis, on the date of Leonardo's death, was far from the scene, at the court of Saint-Germain-en-Laye near Paris. But Vasari's point was still made—the artist was as good as or better than the King, or any other mortal; and by extension, everything that Leonardo had touched was venerable and beyond price. And this was not a viewpoint held by Vasari alone, but by swarms of imitative artists at the time and later. When it developed that the small number of his original works could not satisfy those who questioned his exalted position, innumerable copies and pale reflections of his work came to be accepted as legitimate. As time passed and his beatification became complete, critics and savants of the late 16th, 17th and 18th Centuries were fulsome in their praise of any and every object that might, however tenuously, be associated with the master.

The reaction was inevitable and healthy. John Ruskin, the brilliant 19th Century British essayist and professor of fine arts, had the courage to suggest that Leonardo had been, after all, only a man and that his paintings, like those of other artists, consisted simply of colors applied to a surface. Ruskin lacked the critical apparatus to differentiate between the imitative and the genuine; he did appreciate the quality of Leonardo's work, but made plain that he thought the master was much overrated—had been, in fact, "the slave of an archaic smile." The French Impressionist Pierre-Auguste Renoir was more blunt. "Leonardo da Vinci bores me," he said. "He ought to have stuck to his flying machines. His Apostles and Christ are all sentimental. I am very sure that these Jewish fishermen could risk their skins for their faith without needing to look like dying ducks in a thunderstorm." Renoir's was an understandable reaction; and high time.

Perhaps the most dramatic change in attitude toward Leonardo's image occurred early in this century when the artist fell under the heavy, humorless scrutiny of Sigmund Freud. Working with what he took to be historical facts, Freud in 1910 produced his celebrated essay *Leonardo da Vinci, and a Memory of His Childhood*. In it he conjectured that Leonardo, lacking a father image in the first years of his life, had more-than-normal erotic relations with his mother, the peasant Caterina; and later on, when he was brought into his father's household, Leonardo received extreme affection from his childless stepmother. Freud also placed great emphasis on a childhood dream or fantasy recorded by the artist himself, involving an erotic encounter with a large bird which alighted on Leonardo's

Though he painted little in his final years, Leonardo remained interested in scientific projects. Enjoying the hospitality of Francis I in France, he made the study reproduced above for a plan to channel water from the Loire River to the town of Romorantin, where the King had commissioned him to design a palace and gardens. The project never came to fruition, but some of his ideas were later used in building the lovely castle of Chambord.

cradle. Coupling this with remarks of Leonardo such as "the act of procreation and everything that has any relation to it is so disgusting that human beings would soon die out if there were no pretty faces and sensuous dispositions," Freud concluded that in all likelihood Leonardo was a latent homosexual who sublimated his inclinations in his voracious seeking after knowledge.

In his analysis, Freud made the error, surprising in a scholar, of accepting material in the widely read book by Dmitri Merejkowski, *The Romance of Leonardo da Vinci,* a work of almost unadulterated fiction. In addition Freud used an erroneous translation of Leonardo's notes, in which the bird in the childhood fantasy was rendered as "vulture." Using this mistranslation as a point of departure, Freud then embarked on a lengthy, involved discussion of ancient Egyptian sexual-religious beliefs concerning vultures. After noting that the Egyptians had worshiped a motherly, vulture-headed goddess named *Mut,* Freud asked solemnly: "We may question whether the sound similarity to our word 'mother' *(Mutter)* is only coincidental?"

The proper translation of the word is actually not "vulture" but "kite," a bird of the hawk family common in Europe, and thus Freud's excursion into the lore of vultures becomes quite irrelevant. Beyond that, Freud was unaware of the true chronology of Leonardo's paintings and therefore made some gross blunders in trying to relate his own psychological observations to the works of art which he discussed.

Freud himself was dubious about the ultimate value of his essay—"I would not like you to judge the certainty of our other results by this sample," he later wrote, and if he were now alive he might well withdraw or greatly revise it. The work has been repeatedly attacked and disparaged by later scholars, psychiatrists and art historians, with considerable justification. However, parts of Freud's analysis remain as valuable contributions to any study of Leonardo. Notably, Freud enabled others to see the complex, looming genius as a human being, flawed or fallible as the case may be.

The immediate response to this critical trend, particularly among artists, was one of great release. The *Mona Lisa,* in her position of remote authority in the Louvre, became the object of one of the most simple, subtle and devastating lampoons in all art. Marcel Duchamp, already then a leading iconoclast of the art world, placed on exhibition a copy of the *Mona Lisa*—adorned with a beard and moustache. With this, the overidealized, ethereal vision of Leonardo at last collapsed. Thereafter it became possible to regard the magnificent qualities of the artist and the man on their own terms.

A sound means of ensuring a clear view is to note carefully what Leonardo has to say about himself on the various questions one may wish to ask. What, for example, was his religious belief—or had he any? Vasari, his biographer, raises a small smoke screen in this regard. In the first edition of his *Lives of the Painters,* published in 1550, he wrote that "Leonardo was of such a heretical frame of mind that he did not adhere to any kind of religion, believing that it is perhaps better to be a philosopher than a Christian." In the second edition (1568) he omitted the sentence, leaving the reader with this picture of the old man on his deathbed: "He desired to occupy himself with the truths of the Catholic faith and the holy Christian religion. Then, having confessed and shown his penitence with much lamentation, he devoutly took the Sacrament."

The sentence was doubtless stricken because Vasari was anxious to project what he thought was a better image of Leonardo. But it is more revealing to observe that in his will Leonardo made elaborate stipulations concerning his Christian funeral. There were to be three high Masses and 30 low at four separate churches; a procession of monks and mourners, bearing torches or candles, was to light him on his way. (Forty pounds of wax for the candles, ordered the meticulous artist.) In contrast to this, in one of his "prophecies" or riddles, Leonardo had written: "Of the dead who are taken to be buried: The simple folk will carry a great number of lights to illuminate the journeys of all those who have wholly lost the power of sight. O human folly! O madness of mankind!" Thus certainly he was scornful of the abuses of the Church and was an intellectual forerunner of the Reformation. (It was in 1517, while Leonardo was in residence at Amboise, that Martin Luther nailed his 95 theses to the door of the church at Wittenberg, although it is unlikely that Leonardo ever learned of them.)

However, this is by no means to suggest that Leonardo was an atheist. The name of the Creator appears often enough in his writings to indicate that he had some undefined but still enduring conception of a divine power. If he had wished to be explicit about it, as he was explicit in so many other matters, nothing would have prevented him; yet apparently he remained silent. In regard to death he left a passage of great lyric beauty, and perhaps it was this that he had in mind when the end came:

"See: one's hopes and wishes to return to one's homeland and origin —they are just as moths trying to reach the light. And the man who is looking forward with joyful curiosity to the new spring, and the new summer, and always new months and new years—and even if the time he is longing for ever comes, it will always seem to him to be too late—he does not notice that his longing carries within it the germs of his own death.

"But this longing is the quintessence, the spirit of the elements, which through the soul is enclosed in the human body and which craves for return to its source. You must know that this very yearning is the quintessence of life, the handmaid of Nature, and that Man is a model of the world."

There are curious ambiguities in Leonardo's attitude toward violence and despotism. Of his gentleness and reverence for life there can be no question; but he was also capable of designing the most murderous, even diabolical of weapons—and of drawing them so beautifully that his work sheets are fine works of art. In looking at his drawings of scythed chariots or the manufacture of huge cannon one almost forgets that the purpose of these devices was to kill. It is easy enough, and correct, to point to the general savagery of the times, to Leonardo's necessity of securing patronage and to his strong love of liberty. That theme is recurrent in his writings: "When besieged by ambitious tyrants I find a means of offense and defense in order to preserve the chief gift of Nature, which is liberty." Yet Leonardo voluntarily entered the service of the most ambitious tyrant of all, Cesare Borgia, whose chief purpose was to take away the liberty of others. It is fruitless to ask why Leonardo committed himself to such apparently incompatible employment; all that emerges is another aspect of the larger mystery of the man.

Money was a concern for Leonardo during much of his life, although he seems never to have been in actual want and at various times was rather well-off. But something compelled him to keep the most picayune accounts of household expenses—one is likely to find on a sheet containing some lovely drawing or deep artistic concept a list of the pennies he spent for pots and pans. While he was painting the *Last Supper* he made no dated notes about the work, his progress or his feelings; instead he set down something that must have been important to him, although it reads like the ledger entry of a small-minded merchant: "Monday I bought [a piece] of cloth, 13 lire, 14½ soldi, on the 17th day of October, 1497." Leonardo's asceticism is well known; his writings are full of observations such as "Intellectual passion drives out sensuality. . . . Wine is good, but water is preferable at table. . . . Small rooms or dwellings set the mind in the right path, large ones cause it to go astray. . . . Whoso curbs not lustful desires puts himself on a level with the beasts. . . . If you want money in abundance, you will end by not enjoying it." In contradiction to this, there were Leonardo's wildly optimistic schemes for obtaining sudden riches, as with the booty from the uncaptured Turkish fleet, or the machine he invented (but never built) for making needles, with all the figures on the fortune this might bring. And to contradict the contradiction there is this: "He who wishes to become rich in a day is hanged in a year."

As he aged, Leonardo's dark view of mankind and his general pessimism became increasingly pronounced. Occasionally he would erupt in outbursts which in their fury and scatological phrasing are like those of Jonathan Swift's castigations of men "who can call themselves nothing more than a passage for food, producers of dung, fillers up of privies, for of them nothing else appears in the world, nor is there any virtue in them, for nothing of them remains but full privies." Yet to the end of his life, at least to those immediately around him, Leonardo displayed the gentle sweetness described by Vasari. Among the very few human documents concerning him that survive there is a letter written by Francesco Melzi shortly after his death. It is addressed to Leonardo's

Among the vast collection of notes which Leonardo brought to Cloux were these three studies on the principle of perpetual motion. The concept had plagued inventors for centuries, and although Leonardo had already proved that it was mechanically impossible to produce such a machine, he toyed with the idea. His drawings, which may simply have pleased him for their elegant geometry, show that he considered making a wheel turn by keeping it in constant imbalance—in two cases with weights which rolled back and forth in curved channels between rim and hub, in a third with weights which, overbalancing and striking a stop, moved a ratcheted wheel.

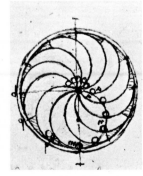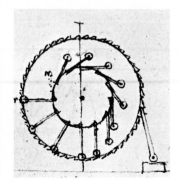

half-brothers: "I believe that the death of your brother, Maestro Leonardo, had already been certified to you. To me he was the best of fathers, and it is impossible for me to express the grief that his death has caused me. Until the day when my body is laid under the ground, I shall experience perpetual sorrow, and not without reason, for he daily showed me the most devoted and warmest affection. . . . His loss is a grief to everyone, for it is not in the power of nature to reproduce another such man."

There remains the question of Leonardo's inability to bring so many of his projects to conclusion. If one wishes a psychoanalytic view, there is Freud's. During the first few years of his life, Freud's thesis runs, Leonardo was abandoned by his father; consequently when he became a man, Leonardo abandoned his own "children," his works. But perhaps Leonardo's own comments afford a better explanation: he suggested that his undertakings were so many and so diverse that he simply could not make an end of them.

Upon Leonardo's death the stricken young Francesco Melzi found himself the possessor of "the infinite number of volumes" of Leonardo's papers. He took them all to his home at Vaprio d'Adda near Milan where long afterward, in 1566, Vasari saw them and noted that Melzi guarded them "as though they were [religious] relics." Thus, until Melzi's death in 1570, the manuscripts and drawings were in safe but fairly inactive hands. Melzi did select and copy a small fraction of them, doing his best to extract from the great "collection without order" at least one book—the *Treatise on Painting,* on which Leonardo had worked for the last 25 years of his life but which he left unfinished. As will presently be seen, Melzi's compilation was of inestimable value. Aside from that work, however, he acted merely as a custodian. He wrote no commentary on Leonardo or the papers and never revealed whatever he may have known of Leonardo's intentions concerning their organization, although he had possession of the legacy for half a century. The thought of his long inactivity has caused many Leonardo scholars to grind their teeth. Be that as it may, the fact is that Melzi preserved the papers and drawings intact and left them to his lawyer son, Orazio, trusting that the latter would have the same regard for them as he had. Sadly, Orazio did not, and soon the process of dispersal began. The manuscripts and unbound sheets were bought, stolen, given away, sold and scattered over half the world in the ensuing centuries. Today the principal fragments may be found in Milan, Venice and Turin; in Paris; and in Windsor, London, and the library of the Earl of Leicester at Holkham Hall. Smaller pieces and individual pages have come to rest in private and public collections everywhere—in the U.S., material that must once have been in Melzi's hands can be seen in New York's Metropolitan Museum and in the private collections of John Nicholas Brown and Robert Lehman. It is impossible to say how much has been lost. Half the total? Even more? Some may still be recovered; for example, around the beginning of the 19th Century a great number of pages somehow disappeared from the possession of the British Crown. The probability is that these have not been destroyed but have only been hidden.

Of the many men who dispersed Leonardo's written legacy only two are worth mentioning, the sculptor Pompeo Leoni and Napoleon Bonaparte. Late in the 16th Century, Leoni got hold of a large number of the papers and attacked them with scissors, assembling two scrapbooks which he then sold. One of these, called the *Codex Atlanticus* because of its great size (1,222 pages), consists mainly of scientific material bundled together without order; it is now the treasured possession of the Biblioteca Ambrosiana in Milan. The other is made up of small illustrations, artistic in interest, which Leoni snipped out of the *Codex Atlanticus* and other papers, and mounted on fresh sheets; today they are preserved in the British Royal Collection at Windsor Castle. If scholars have an occasional harsh word for Francesco Melzi, one can easily imagine their comments on Leoni.

Napoleon's part in the dispersal did no real harm; at least nothing was mutilated. Rather, it is amusing—if the word may be applied to grand theft—because of a remark he made at the time. When he entered Milan with his conquering army in 1796 he seized not only the *Codex Atlanticus* but a dozen other Leonardo manuscripts as well, sending them to Paris with the explanation that "all men of genius . . . are French, whatever the country which has given them birth." At the end of the Napoleonic Wars the *Codex Atlanticus* was returned to Milan, but the other manuscripts are still in the Institut de France, in Paris.

In the tragedy of the loss and scattering of Leonardo's papers there is at least one happy note—the effort of Francesco Melzi to salvage the *Treatise on Painting*. Melzi, as he indicated at the end of his compilation, extracted material from 18 of Leonardo's "books," and of these compilations by the master, two thirds have disappeared. Thus, through Melzi's efforts—and it is safe to assume that the extracts were faithfully copied by the devout pupil—we have today many of Leonardo's thoughts on painting that might otherwise have vanished. Melzi's compilation is disorganized and he seems to have been unable to summon up the intellectual stamina to complete it; he searched through the papers and grouped together, under such headings as studio practice, drapery, light and shade, clouds and the horizon, whatever he thought appropriate. (Recent research, notably that of Carlo Pedretti, an Italian scholar now working in the U.S., indicates that Melzi followed procedures laid down or suggested by the erratic master himself.) The *Treatise* is therefore difficult reading and the despair of editors who would prefer to see it methodically arranged. Nonetheless it is, as Sir Kenneth Clark suggests, "the most precious document in the whole history of art." There is no similar work in which a great artist addresses himself in such detail to others who are to follow him. As he made his scattered notes for the *Treatise* Leonardo drew on the writings of predecessors such as Leon Battista Alberti and even the drearily practical Cennino Cennini, whose *Craftsman's Handbook* he had known in his youth; but he added insights and advice that only he could have conceived. For example, long before it became fashionable to probe the psychological motivation of artists, Leonardo trenchantly warned the painter against viewing the world too subjectively, for he would then paint the same subject over and over again: one that resembles himself, because his narcissistic "soul," or subconscious, can see nothing different or more attractive.

The earliest printed editions of the *Treatise,* in Italian and French, date from 1651. For reasons still unknown, they do not follow Melzi's rendition but are based on an abridged version whose origin is obscure. It was not until 1817, after Melzi's version was rediscovered in the Vatican Library, that the *Treatise* was printed in the version familiar today. It has been published many times in many languages, and each new publication has caused excitement and stimulation that continue into our own time. For example, there is room for his ideas in 20th Century painting, which may strike one as at the farthest remove from Leonardo's art. Thus, in *Cahiers d'Art,* the Surrealist painter Max Ernst in 1937 wrote of the "unbearable visual obsession" that resulted, as it had in the case of Victor Hugo, from his application of Leonardo's advice concerning the study of stains on walls. And French writers in 1912 defended the multifaceted paintings of Cubism with a quotation from the *Treatise:* "We know well that sight, through rapid observation, discovers in one glance an infinity of forms; nonetheless, it can only take in one thing at a time."

As influential as the *Treatise* has been, however, Leonardo's impact on art arose from a much broader base. So broad was it, indeed, that he himself did not see it objectively and never wrote about it. It had nothing to do with his individual motifs or compositions, finished or unfinished. Rather, it was his basic conception of scale and proportion. Such words are not easily defined; at best one can say that one thing is larger or smaller than another, or that it is well- or ill-proportioned. But in Leonardo's case it is not a question of relative size or of value-judgments concerning shapes. It is simply that Leonardo's figures belong to a new race, larger and grander than those of such painters as Botticelli or Pollaiuolo. They are bulkier, weightier, more massive than those of the Early Renaissance. This new conception of majesty, evident first in the *Last Supper* (begun when Michelangelo was 20 and Raphael only 12), changed Western art forever. With it the High Renaissance began, and every artist who was to follow became Leonardo's debtor.

Leonardo, the lover and creator of mystery, was buried among princes and counselors at Amboise. In the turmoil of the following years, the Huguenot Wars and the Revolution, the cemetery in which he lay became a ruin. Headstones were uprooted and used for building material; even the lead coffins were melted down, and the bones of the dead were intermingled. In the early 19th Century the French Romantic poet Arsène Houssaye tried to recover the remains of the artist from a communal burial heap. Knowing that Leonardo had been a tall man and an intellectual, Houssaye assembled fragments that seemed likely: a large skull and massive bones. Today these are entombed in a small chapel beside the castle, where the tourist guide insists that they are Leonardo's, although probably they are not. Thus it was contrived, three centuries after his death, that a final mystery should surround him. The bones may be those of two men, ten men, or, in symbol, of all men who make bold journeys in this world.

The Final Trumpet

Leonardo da Vinci was probably 62 years old when he drew the self-portrait shown here, and his spirit must have been much as he caused his likeness to be: older than his years, disillusioned, weary. He had done so much, and yet had realized so little: without a home, without a patron, he was about to wander, almost forgotten, into his old age. Even his likeness would survive only in this one picture; and of it one can only say, with melancholy truthfulness, that it is remarkably unrevealing. "This great furrowed mountain of a face," wrote Sir Kenneth Clark four centuries later, "with its noble brow, commanding cavernous eyes, and undulating foothills of beard is like the faces of all the great men of the nineteenth Century as the camera has preserved them for us—Darwin, Tolstoy, Walt Whitman. Time, with its spectacle of human suffering, has reduced them all to a common level of venerability." Leonardo, with five years of his life still to live, apparently saw himself as an anonymous old man.

Thus it was that he arrived in France, almost as a ward of the young King, Francis I, who out of great respect for an intellectual and artistic giant of his age had offered him a haven. And here in an alien land, he came to the end of his days, amidst the dying echoes of his final trumpet blast: the apocalyptic series of drawings called *The Deluge* which, in his prediction, would one day inundate the earth and end the world of man.

The only known authentic likeness of Leonardo, this red-chalk drawing was done by him in his last years in Italy. At the bottom of the picture is an inscription, added by a later hand: "Leonardo da Vinci, portrait of himself as an old man."

Self-Portrait, c. 1514

172

Pierre Dumonstier, after Jean Clouet:
Francis I, 16th Century

To Leonardo, who had worked for so many patrons over so many years, the place to which Francis I invited him must have seemed a haven indeed. Beset as he had been with anxieties in his last years in Rome, he now found himself treated with the greatest liberality, yet with nothing asked in return but to talk with the King, as the King pleased, about matters that interested them both. For this was a monarch of far-ranging interests, the ruler of a country as

lively and restless and burgeoning as his own spirit. An adventurer and conqueror by nature, Francis was as bent on adding cultural wealth to France as he was on adding territories. And to him Leonardo was the fountain of all wisdom—the greatest authority in history on painting, sculpture and architecture, and equally profound in matters of philosophy in which the King sought his advice.

It was a bustling haven, too, with a lively court filling the great castle at Amboise in whose great looming shadow Leonardo's manor house stood. Though he participated little in court affairs, he could do so when he chose, and doubtless he did take part in some festivities from time to time. But more often, he worked with his own thoughts and his own affairs, perhaps occasionally pausing to gaze upon, and sketch, the many-gabled walls which were protecting him in these quiet years.

Attributed to Leonardo: Drawing of the castle at Amboise, c. 1518

The manor house of Cloux where Leonardo spent
his final years has survived the centuries and today
has been restored, in many respects, to approximately the
state in which he knew it. Now owned by Count Hubert
de Saint-Bris, it serves as a monument to the artist,
and tourists walking through its gardens can well imagine
the old man sitting there, for here are the same scenes that he
saw. His bedroom *(left, above)*, however, is now filled
with furniture of later centuries; the bed he died in has long
since disappeared. But the kitchen *(center)*, frequently

Exterior view of Cloux

the center of life in the winter period, is much the same as it was. Even a stretch of the tunnel connecting the manor house with the castle at Amboise has been preserved. Through it Francis I, his youthful patron-king, often came on his many visits to talk philosophy and art with the wise old man whose opinion on all matters he respected so highly.

Of his work in those last years at Cloux, it can at best be said that Leonardo puttered about at the things that interested him the most. Except for the Loire canal project at Romorantin, the King did not burden him with

commissions; but probably, from time to time, Leonardo did contribute, with drawings or designs, to some of the court's festivities, as he had so many years before at Sforza's court in Milan: one such was the mechanical lion whose breast could open to reveal a field of lilies. He did no paintings, but the drawings from this period are still firm and clear. They show almost no effects of the partial paralysis he suffered after a minor stroke. Such were his final years, in a setting which, for all the fact that he was a virtual exile, may well have become dear to him.

St. John the Baptist, c. 1515

The personal possessions which Leonardo had at Cloux were, when one considers the richness of his life and years, pitifully few. There was his vast collection of notes and sketches; after his death, these were taken into zealous guardianship by his young friend, Francesco Melzi. There were his books; these have been lost, but in his notes he details some of those he read in his lifetime: Titus Livius' *Decades;* Leon Battista Alberti's treatise on architecture; Aulus Cornelius Celsus' *De Medicina;* Plutarch's *Lives;* Pliny's *Natural History;* Seneca; Euclid; the Bible. In all, that list includes some 37 titles from all fields of human knowledge. Those shown here are editions from Leonardo's time, carefully collected in recent years; he may have had copies of these same works at Cloux.

Of his paintings, he had only three: the *Mona Lisa,* the *St. Anne* and that strange work of his late years, the *St. John (above).* Disturbing as it is, this soft figure with the provocative smile must be accepted as Leonardo's personal interpretation of the Baptist who traditionally was conceived as a fiery, gaunt ascetic. Certainly, in this curving, smiling pose, Leonardo expresses the quintessence of the eternal mystery which is so much a part of his work—the enigma of creation and of life itself. It is not difficult to imagine that, when the old man died, his eyes were fixed on that upraised finger and that enigmatic smile.

179

A Tumult of Waters
To End the World

Throughout his life, Leonardo was obsessed with the movement of water, and there were many occasions when he turned this interest to useful ends. But toward the end of his years this fascination seems at times to have overwhelmed him, and from these moments came his strange and fearsome drawings of the Deluge which he predicted would someday sweep away man and all his works and end the world. Almost abstract, and daring in their abandonment of conventional art forms, these profound and vivid exercises of his imagination show the most

basic tenets of his art—his passion for complex and twisting movements and for rounded forms—as well as his fear for the future of mankind. His scientific knowledge is applied here with devastating logic to show how puny are the means of man when pitted against nature: here a prodigious mind is dredging the very bottom of an anguished soul. "Ah, what dreadful tumults one heard resounding through the gloomy air!" he wrote in the commentary which described these drawings. "Ah me, how many lamentations!"

"Among irremediable and destructive
terrors the inundations caused by rivers
in flood should certainly be set before every
other dreadful and terrifying movement,"
wrote Leonardo; and so it is not surprising
that his last major endeavor should be
the series of Deluge drawings in which a
gigantic, rolling mass of water crashes
upon the cowering world. His descriptions
of how to depict a Deluge are no less
terrifying than the nightmare scenes he
drew: "Let the dark, gloomy air be seen
beaten by the rush of opposing winds
wreathed in perpetual rain mingled with
hail. . . . All around let there be seen
ancient trees uprooted and torn in pieces by
the fury of the winds. . . . And let the
fragments of some of the mountains be
fallen down into the depths of one of the
valleys, and there form a barrier to the
swollen waters of its river, which having
already burst the barrier rushes on with
immense waves. . . ."

This was Leonardo's Last Judgment.
Whether he meant it to constitute his
final message to mankind, no one can say;
but the Deluge series affords insight into
the preoccupation of his lifetime. The
overpowering forces of nature at first
intrigued, then fascinated and, finally,
apparently terrified him.

Deluge II, 1514-1516

APPENDIX

Chronology: Painters of the 15th and 16th Centuries

Leonardo's predecessors and contemporaries are grouped here in chronological order according to school (Florence, Venice, etc.) or country.

The colored bands correspond to the life-spans of the painters or, where this information is unknown, to the periods when they flourished (fl.).

1400   1500   1600

FLORENCE
UCCELLO 1397-1475
FRA ANGELICO c. 1400-1455
MASACCIO c. 1401-1428
FRA FILIPPO LIPPI 1406-1469
CASTAGNO c. 1410-1457
DOM. VENEZIANO c. 1410-1461
BENOZZO GOZZOLI c. 1420-1497
BALDOVINETTI 1425-1499
A. DEL POLLAIUOLO c. 1431-1498
VERROCCHIO 1435-1488
COSIMO ROSSELLI 1439-1507
BOTTICELLI c. 1444-1510
GHIRLANDAIO 1449-1494
LEONARDO DA VINCI 1452-1519
FILIPPINO LIPPI 1457-1504
LORENZO DI CREDI c. 1459-1537
PIERO DI COSIMO 1462-1521
FRA BARTOLOMMEO 1472-1517
MICHELANGELO 1475-1564
ANDREA DEL SARTO 1486-1531
ROSSO FIORENTINO 1494-1540
PONTORMO c. 1494-1557
BRONZINO c. 1503-1572

VENICE
JACOPO BELLINI c. 1400-1470
ANTONIO VIVARINI c. 1415-1484
BARTOLOMMEO VIVARINI fl. 1450-1498
GENTILE BELLINI c. 1429-1507
GIOVANNI BELLINI c. 1430-1516
ANTONELLO DA MESSINA c. 1430-1479
CARLO CRIVELLI c. 1435-1495
ALVISE VIVARINI c. 1446-1502
CARPACCIO c. 1455-1526
TITIAN 1477-1576
GIORGIONE c. 1478-1510
PALMA VECCHIO 1480-1528
LORENZO LOTTO 1480-1556
SEBASTIANO DEL PIOMBO 1485-1547
JACOPO BASSANO 1510-1592
TINTORETTO 1518-1594
PAOLO VERONESE 1528-1588

SIENA
SASSETTA c. 1392-1450
GIOVANNI DI PAOLO 1403-1482
VECCHIETTA 1412-1480
MATTEO DI GIOVANNI c. 1430-1495
FRANCESCO DI GIORGIO 1439-1502
NEROCCIO DI LANDI 1447-1500
SODOMA 1477-1549
BECCAFUMI c. 1486-1551

CENTRAL ITALY
PIERO DELLA FRANCESCA c. 1416-1492
MELOZZO DA FORLI 1438-1494
SIGNORELLI c. 1441-1523
PERUGINO 1445-1523
PINTURICCHIO 1454-1513
RAPHAEL 1483-1520
GIULIO ROMANO 1492-1546
VASARI 1511-1574

1400   1500   1600

1400   1500   1600

NORTHERN ITALY
PISANELLO 1395-1455
FOPPA c. 1427-1516
COSIMO TURA 1430-1495
MANTEGNA 1431-1506
COSSA c. 1435-1477
AMBROGIO DA PREDIS 1455-1522
BOLTRAFFIO 1467-1516
MARCO D'OGGIONO 1475-1530
CESARE DA SESTO 1477-1523
DOSSO DOSSI c. 1479-1542
LUINI c. 1480-1532
CORREGGIO 1494-1534
MORETTO c. 1498-1555
PARMIGIANINO 1503-1540
MORONI c. 1525-1578

FRANCE
FOUQUET c. 1420-1481
FROMENT fl. 1450-1490
MAÎTRE DE MOULINS fl. c. 1480-1500
JEAN CLOUET c. 1475-1547

GERMANY
MEISTER FRANCKE fl. c. 1410-1435
STEPHAN LOCHNER fl. c. 1420-1451
LUCAS MOSER fl. 1431-1440
KONRAD WITZ (SWISS) fl. 1433-1447
MULTSCHER c. 1400-1467
SCHONGAUER c. 1430-1491
PACHER c. 1435-1498
HANS HOLBEIN, THE ELDER 1460-1524
GRÜNEWALD c. 1470-1530
ALBRECHT DÜRER 1471-1528
CRANACH, THE ELDER 1472-1553
BURGKMAIR 1473-1531
ALBRECHT ALTDORFER c. 1480-1538
HANS BALDUNG GRIEN 1480-1545
HANS HOLBEIN, THE YOUNGER 1497-1543

FLANDERS
CAMPIN 1375-1444
ROGER VAN DER WEYDEN c. 1399-1464
PETRUS CHRISTUS c. 1410-1472
DIRCK BOUTS c. 1420-1475
MEMLING c. 1430-1494
HUGO VAN DER GOES c. 1440-1482
JEROME BOSCH c. 1450-1516
GERARD DAVID c. 1450-1523
QUINTEN MASSYS c. 1466-1530
GOSSAERT (MABUSE) c. 1470-1533
PATINIR c. 1475-1524
VAN SCOREL 1495-1562
PIETER BRUEGHEL, THE ELDER c. 1525-1569

HOLLAND
LUCAS VAN LEYDEN 1494-1533
HEEMSKERCK 1498-1574
AERTSEN 1508-1575
ANTONIS MOR (MORO) c. 1519-1576

SPAIN
MARTORELL fl. 1433-1453
BERMEJO fl. 1474-1495
MORALES 1509-1586
COELLO c. 1515-1590
EL GRECO c. 1542-1614

1400   1500   1600

Benois Madonna, begun 1478

Three Controversial Madonnas

Of the few paintings in existence which can be attributed to Leonardo, these three Madonnas have over the centuries excited the greatest controversy. All three belong to his early years, but the degree to which they have been worked on since by others has almost obliterated the traces characteristic of his youthful hand. Yet all three of them can be definitely attributed to him through sketches or drawings.

The *Benois Madonna (left)*, now in The Hermitage in Leningrad, shows no qualities of Leonardo in any of its elements: it is heavily overpainted. What traces there may once have been of a Leonardesque landscape have long been lost, and even important parts of the composition are singularly unimpressive. "The baby was always monstrous," wrote Clark, "and the drapery of the sleeve laboured." But the several drawings for the painting, unquestionably by Leonardo, show a freshness and originality which clearly stamp it as an immature example of his developing, classic style.

The *Litta Madonna (lower left)* was probably taken to Milan by Leonardo in an unfinished state, having been begun about 1480. It was later twice completely repainted—once in 1495 by a Milanese artist, and again in the 19th Century when it was transferred from the original wood panel to canvas. From drawings, it can be established that Leonardo probably designed the pose and finished the Virgin's head and part of the Child's body. The *Virgin with Flowers (below)*, probably a student exercise of Leonardo's apprenticeship with Verrocchio, can be traced through numerous parts—the Virgin's plaited hair, her left hand, the drapery, the flowers—which are entirely in the style of Leonardo's *Annunciation*, now in the Uffizi.

Litta Madonna, begun c. 1480

Virgin with Flowers, begun c. 1473

Catalogue of Illustrations *Unless otherwise noted, all dimensions are in inches.*

BALDOVINETTI, ALESSO: 1425-1499, Florentine. P.42-43: *Annunciation,* tempera on panel, 51 x $133\frac{1}{2}$, San Miniato al Monte, Florence.

BOTTICELLI, SANDRO: c.1444-1510, Florentine. P.43: *St. Augustine in His Study,* fresco, 71 x 47, Ognissanti, Florence.

CAPROTTI, GIAN GIACOMO DE' (SALAI): 1480-1523/24, Milanese. P.143: *Mona Lisa* copy, oil, $30\frac{3}{10}$ x $20\frac{9}{10}$, Collection Dr. Carl Muller, Thalwil, Switzerland.

CASTAGNO, ANDREA DEL: c.1410-1457, Florentine. P.96-97: *Last Supper,* fresco, 13'0" x 28'4", S. Apollonia, Florence.

CHAMPAIGNE, PHILIPPE DE (?): 1602-1674, French. P.142: *Mona Lisa* copy, oil, $32\frac{1}{10}$ x $22\frac{3}{5}$, Nasjonalgalleriet, Oslo.

CREDI, LORENZO DI (?): c.1459-1537, Florentine. P.38: *Portrait of Verrocchio,* tempera on panel, 23 x 18, Uffizi Gallery, Florence.

De Sphaera, miniature. P.23, 7 x $5\frac{1}{2}$, Biblioteca Estense, Modena.

DUMONSTIER, PIERRE, L'ONCLE: French. P.174: *Francis I* (After Jean Clouet), colored pencil, $13\frac{2}{3}$ x $9\frac{2}{3}$, Bibliothèque Nationale, Paris.

GHIRLANDAIO, DOMENICO: 1449-1494, Florentine. P.43: *St. Jerome in His Study,* fresco, 71 x 47, Ognissanti, Florence.

Grammatica di Donato, miniatures. P.62-63, Biblioteca Trivulziana, Milan.

Early Christian *Last Supper.* P.94, Mosaic, Sant' Apollinare Nuovo, Ravenna.

LEONARDO: 1452-1519, Florentine. Cover: Detail of *Mona Lisa,* oil on panel, $30\frac{3}{10}$ x $20\frac{9}{10}$, Musée du Louvre, Paris. Front end paper: *Allegory,* red chalk on brownish gray paper, $6\frac{2}{3}$ x 11, Royal Collection, Windsor Castle. P.8: Sketch of a young woman pointing, black chalk, $8\frac{1}{2}$ x 4, Royal Collection, Windsor Castle. P.13: Study of a star-of-Bethlehem, red chalk and pen and ink, $7\frac{3}{4}$ x $6\frac{1}{4}$, Royal Collection, Windsor Castle. P.16: Grotesque head, Scaramuccia, charcoal, $15\frac{3}{8}$ x 11, Christ Church, Oxford. P.24: Sketch of the hanged Baroncelli, pen and ink, $7\frac{1}{2}$ x 3, Musée Bonnat, Bayonne. P.26: *St. Jerome,* panel, $40\frac{1}{2}$ x $21\frac{1}{2}$, Musei Vaticani, Rome. P.31: Drawing of a Unicorn, pen and ink, $3\frac{2}{3}$ x $3\frac{1}{6}$, Ashmolean Museum, Oxford. P.33: *Antique Warrior,* silverpoint on cream-colored surface, $11\frac{1}{4}$ x $8\frac{1}{8}$, British Museum, London. P.34: Drawing of an old man and a youth, red chalk, $8\frac{1}{4}$ x $5\frac{7}{8}$, Uffizi Gallery, Florence. P.44: Landscape, detail from Verrocchio's *Baptism of Christ,* Uffizi Gallery, Florence. P.45: Kneeling angel in profile, detail from Verrocchio's *Baptism of Christ.* P.46-47: *Annunciation,* panel, $38\frac{1}{2}$ x 86, Uffizi Gallery, Florence. P.48: *Arno Landscape,* pen and ink, $7\frac{1}{2}$ x 11, Uffizi Gallery, Florence. P.49: *Ginevra de' Benci,* panel, $16\frac{1}{2}$ x $14\frac{1}{2}$, National Gallery of Art, Washington, D.C. P.50: *Madonna of the Rocks,* panel, transferred to canvas, 78 x 48, Musée du Louvre, Paris. P.51: *Madonna of the Rocks,* panel, 75 x 47, National Gallery, London. P.52: *Lady with an Ermine,* panel, $21\frac{1}{2}$ x 16, Museum Czartoryski, Cracow. P.54: Drawing of a lute, pen and ink on parchment, $5\frac{11}{12}$ x $8\frac{1}{4}$, Bibliothèque Nationale, Paris. P.56: Mask, pen and ink, $2\frac{2}{3}$ x $2\frac{2}{3}$, Royal Collection, Windsor Castle. P.58: Cross-sectional anatomy of the leg, pen and brown ink, $11\frac{1}{4}$ x $8\frac{3}{4}$, Royal Collection, Windsor Castle. P.59: Polyhedron, pen and ink, $4\frac{3}{4}$ x $4\frac{4}{5}$, Biblioteca Ambrosiana, Milan. P.64: A horseman trampling on a fallen foe; study for *The Horse,* silverpoint on blue prepared surface, 6 x 7, Royal Collection, Windsor Castle. P.65: A horse and its forelegs; study for *The Horse,* silverpoint on blue prepared surface, $8\frac{1}{2}$ x 6, Royal Collection, Windsor Castle. P.66-67: Ceiling decoration of the *Sala delle Asse,* fresco, Castello Sforzesco, Milan. P.68: *Portrait of a Musician,* panel, 17 x 12, Pinacoteca Ambrosiana. P.69: Youth with a lance, pen and ink and wash over black chalk, $10\frac{1}{2}$ x 7, Royal Collection, Windsor Castle. P.69: Figure wearing a bodice of interlaced ribbons, black chalk, $8\frac{1}{2}$ x $4\frac{1}{2}$, Royal Collection, Windsor Castle. P.69: Man with a club and shackled feet, black chalk, $7\frac{1}{4}$ x 5, Royal Collection, Windsor Castle. P.70: Knot, engraving after Leonardo, 11 x 9, British Museum, London. P.71: Implements rained down on the earth from the clouds, pen and ink, $4\frac{1}{2}$ x 4, Royal Collection, Windsor Castle. P.72: Rope ladders and pinions for scaling a wall, pen and ink, $11\frac{1}{2}$ x 8, Biblioteca Ambrosiana, Milan. P.72: Detail of a corner tower of a fortress, pen and ink, $8\frac{1}{4}$ x $6\frac{2}{3}$ (whole sheet), Bibliothèque Nationale, Paris. P.72-73: Mortars with explosive projectiles, pen and ink and sepia wash, 8 x 16, Biblioteca Ambrosiana, Milan. P.73: Covered armored car, pen and ink and wash, 4 x 9, British Museum, London. P.76: Mold for casting horse, crayon, $4\frac{1}{4}$ x $5\frac{2}{3}$, Biblioteca Nacional, Madrid. P.76: Device for transporting mold, crayon, $4\frac{4}{5}$ x $3\frac{2}{3}$, Biblioteca Nacional, Madrid. P.77: Plan for casting head and neck of horse, crayon, $4\frac{9}{10}$ x $3\frac{1}{10}$, Biblioteca Nacional, Madrid. P.78: *The Ermine as a Symbol of Purity,* pen and ink, diameter $3\frac{5}{8}$, Fitzwilliam Museum (Clarke collection), Cambridge, England. P.81: Study for the dome of Milan cathedral, pen and ink, 13 x $11\frac{1}{3}$ (whole sheet), Biblioteca Ambrosiana, Milan. P.85: Christ, detail of *Last Supper,* tempera, refectory, Santa Maria delle Grazie, Milan. P.86: Study of an Apostle (probably St. Peter), pen and ink over metalpoint on blue prepared paper, $5\frac{2}{3}$ x $4\frac{1}{2}$, Albertina, Vienna. P.86: Study for Judas, red chalk on red prepared paper, $7\frac{1}{12}$ x $5\frac{11}{12}$ (whole sheet), Royal Collection, Windsor Castle. P.86-87: Study for the *Last Supper,* red chalk, $10\frac{1}{4}$ x $15\frac{1}{3}$, Accademia, Venice. P.87: Study, St. Matthew or St. Bartholomew, red chalk on red prepared paper, $7\frac{7}{12}$ x $5\frac{5}{6}$, Royal Collection, Windsor Castle. P.87: Study for St. James the Greater, red chalk, $9\frac{11}{12}$ x $6\frac{5}{6}$ (whole sheet), Royal Collection, Windsor Castle. P.88-89: *Last Supper,* tempera, 13'10" x 29'$7\frac{1}{2}$", Santa Maria delle Grazie, Milan. P.90: Still-life, detail of *Last Supper.* P.91: St. Philip, detail of *Last Supper.* P.92: Judas, detail of *Last Supper.* P.93: Hand of Judas. P.93: Detail of edge of Judas' sleeve. P.100: Studies of water formations, pen and ink, $11\frac{1}{2}$ x 8, Royal Collection, Windsor Castle. P.103: Embryo in the womb, pen and ink, $11\frac{7}{8}$ x $8\frac{3}{8}$ (whole sheet), Royal Collection, Windsor Castle. P.104: Optics of a mirror, brown ink on paper, 9 x $6\frac{1}{2}$ (whole sheet), British Museum, London. P.106: Water shoes, pen and ink, $10\frac{11}{12}$ x $15\frac{1}{3}$ (whole sheet), Biblioteca Ambrosiana, Milan. P.107: Life preserver, pen and ink, $10\frac{1}{2}$ x $7\frac{1}{4}$ (whole sheet), Biblioteca Ambrosiana, Milan. P.111: Anatomical drawing of a skull facing left, pen and ink, 7 x 5, Royal Collection, Windsor Castle. P.112: Volcanic eruption (possibly a copy), pen and ink and wash, 3 x 3 (whole sheet), Royal Collection, Windsor Castle. P.112: Map of Northern Italy showing the watershed of the Arno, pen and ink and brown wash and blue, $12\frac{1}{2}$ x 17, Royal Collection, Windsor Castle. P.113: Oak leaves with acorns and dyers' greenweed, red chalk on pink surface, touched with white, $7\frac{1}{2}$ x 6, Royal Collection, Windsor Castle. P.114: Chain links, pen and ink, 8 x 5 (whole sheet), Biblioteca Ambrosiana, Milan. P.114: Mechanical car, pen and ink, $10\frac{1}{2}$ x $6\frac{1}{2}$ (whole sheet), Biblioteca Ambrosiana, Milan. P.115: Spinning wheel, pen and ink and brush, 16 x 11 (whole sheet), Biblioteca Ambrosiana, Milan. P.116: Airscrew, pen and ink, 9 x $6\frac{1}{2}$ (whole sheet), Bibliothèque Nationale, Paris. P.116: Flying machine with a man operating it, pen and ink, 9 x $6\frac{1}{2}$ (whole sheet), Bibliothèque Nationale, Paris. P.116-117: Drawing of a flying machine, pen and ink, 9 x $6\frac{1}{2}$ (whole sheet), Bibliothèque Nationale, Paris. P.117: Parachute, pen and ink, 11 x 8 (whole sheet), Biblioteca Ambrosiana, Milan. P.118: Study of the drapery of a woman, silverpoint on red prepared paper, heightened with white, $10\frac{1}{6}$ x $7\frac{2}{3}$, Gabinetto Nationale delle Stampe, Rome. P.120: *Isabella d'Este,* black chalk, charcoal and pastel, reworked by a later hand, $24\frac{7}{8}$ x $18\frac{1}{8}$, Musée du Louvre, Paris. P.122: *Cesare Borgia,* red chalk, $4\frac{1}{3}$ x $11\frac{1}{4}$ (whole sheet), Biblioteca Reale, Turin. P.124: Studies of a male nude, red chalk and pen and ink, $6\frac{1}{4}$ x 6 (whole sheet), Royal Collection, Windsor Castle. P.129: Composition sketch for the *Adoration of the Magi,* pen and ink over metalpoint, $11\frac{1}{4}$ x $8\frac{1}{2}$, Musée du Louvre, Paris. P.130: Studies of single figures, pen and ink, $6\frac{3}{10}$ x $10\frac{1}{5}$ (whole sheet), British Museum, London. P.130: Studies of a Virgin adoring the Infant Christ, pen and ink over metalpoint on pink prepared paper, $7\frac{5}{8}$ x $6\frac{3}{8}$ (whole sheet), The Metropolitan Museum of Art, New York. P.131: Studies of the head and shoulders of a man, pen and ink, $11\frac{1}{3}$ x $7\frac{3}{4}$, Royal Collection, Windsor Castle. P.132: Study of a tree, red chalk, $7\frac{1}{2}$ x 6 (whole sheet), Royal Collection, Windsor Castle. P.132: Study of mountain ranges, red chalk on red prepared surface, heightened with white, $4\frac{1}{6}$ x $6\frac{3}{10}$, Royal Collection, Windsor Castle. P.133: *A Storm over an Alpine Valley,* red chalk, $11\frac{5}{12}$ x $5\frac{11}{12}$, Royal Collection, Windsor Castle. P.134: Perspective study for the background of the *Adoration of the Magi,* pen and ink over metalpoint, with some wash, $6\frac{1}{2}$ x $11\frac{1}{4}$, Uffizi Gallery, Florence. P.134-135: *Adoration of the Magi,* oil on panel, $96\frac{9}{10}$ x $95\frac{7}{8}$, Uffizi Gallery, Florence. P.136-137: Detail of *Adoration of the Magi.* P.138: *Burlington House Cartoon,* black chalk drawing on paper, heightened with white, $54\frac{7}{10}$ x $39\frac{4}{5}$, National Gallery, London. P.139: *Virgin and Child with St. Anne,* oil on panel, $66\frac{9}{10}$ x $50\frac{4}{5}$, Musée du Louvre, Paris. P.140: *Mona Lisa,* oil on panel, $30\frac{3}{10}$ x $20\frac{9}{10}$, Musée du Louvre, Paris. P.140-141: Detail of *Mona Lisa.* P.144: Study for the angel's head in the Louvre *Madonna of the Rocks,* silverpoint on light brown prepared surface, $7\frac{1}{8}$ x $6\frac{1}{4}$, Musée du Louvre, Paris. P.149: Studies for the Trivulzio monument, pen and bister on gray paper, 11 x $7\frac{3}{4}$ (whole sheet), Royal Collection, Windsor Castle. P.153: Study for the head of the *Litta Madonna,* silverpoint on greenish prepared surface, $7\frac{1}{8}$ x $6\frac{5}{8}$, Musée du Louvre, Paris. P.154: Head of a man shouting and a profile; study for the *Battle of Anghiari,* black and red chalk, $7\frac{1}{2}$ x $7\frac{3}{8}$, Museum of Fine Arts, Budapest. P.155: Profile of a man shouting; study for the *Battle of Anghiari,* red chalk, 9 x $7\frac{3}{8}$, Museum of Fine Arts, Budapest. P.156: Study for the *Madonna of the Yarn Winder,* red chalk on pink prepared surface, $8\frac{7}{8}$ x $6\frac{3}{10}$, Royal Collection, Windsor Castle. P.157: *Neptune with Four Sea-Horses,* black chalk, $9\frac{7}{8}$ x $15\frac{1}{2}$, Royal Collection, Windsor Castle. P.158: *Madonna and Child with a Plate of Fruit,* pen and ink over metalpoint, $13\frac{5}{6}$ x $9\frac{5}{6}$, Musée du Louvre, Paris. P.159: *Madonna and Child with a Cat,* recto, pen and ink and wash over a sketch with the stylus, $5\frac{1}{4}$ x $3\frac{3}{4}$, British Museum, London. P.159: *Madonna and Child with a Cat,* verso, pen and ink over a sketch with the stylus, $5\frac{1}{4}$ x $3\frac{3}{4}$, British Museum, London. P.159: *Maiden with a Unicorn,* pen and ink, $3\frac{7}{10}$ x $2\frac{4}{5}$, Ashmolean Museum, Oxford. P.160: Study for *Leda and the Swan,* pen and ink over black chalk, $11\frac{1}{3}$ x 16 (whole sheet), Royal Collection, Windsor Castle. P.160: Study for *Leda and the Swan,* pen and ink over black chalk, $4\frac{7}{8}$ x $4\frac{3}{8}$, Museum Boymans van Beuningen, Rotterdam. P.161: Studies of a woman's head and coiffure, for *Leda and the Swan,* pen and ink over black chalk, $7\frac{7}{8}$ x $6\frac{3}{8}$, Royal Collection, Windsor Castle. P.162: *Apocalyptic Visions (Last Judgment),* pen and ink over black chalk, $11\frac{5}{6}$ x 8, Royal Collection, Windsor Castle. P.165: Course of the Loire, pen and ink, $11\frac{1}{4}$ x $8\frac{1}{6}$ (whole sheet),

Biblioteca Ambrosiana, Milan. P.168: Studies on the principle of perpetual motion, brown ink, each $3\frac{3}{4}$ x $2\frac{3}{4}$, Victoria and Albert Museum, London. P.173: Self-Portrait, red chalk, $13\frac{11}{12}$ x $8\frac{5}{12}$, Biblioteca Reale, Turin. P.174-175: Attributed to Leonardo: Drawing of the castle at Amboise, red chalk, $5\frac{1}{4}$ x $10\frac{1}{5}$, Royal Collection, Windsor Castle. P.179: *St. John the Baptist,* oil on panel, $27\frac{1}{4}$ x $22\frac{1}{2}$, Musée du Louvre. P.180-181: *Hurricane,* pen and ink over black chalk, $6\frac{1}{8}$ x $10\frac{5}{8}$, Royal Collection, Windsor Castle. P.182-183: *Deluge II,* black chalk, yellow and brown ink, $6\frac{3}{8}$ x 8, Royal Collection, Windsor Castle. P.185: *Benois Madonna,* oil, transferred from wood to canvas, $18\frac{7}{8}$ x $12\frac{3}{8}$, The Hermitage, Leningrad. P.185: *Litta Madonna,* oil, transferred from wood to canvas, $16\frac{1}{2}$ x 13, The Hermitage, Leningrad. P.185: *Virgin with Flowers,* oil on wood, $24\frac{1}{2}$ x $18\frac{1}{2}$, Bayerische Staatsgemaeldesammlungen, Munich. Back end paper: Sheet of studies, pen and ink, $12\frac{5}{8}$ x $17\frac{1}{2}$, Royal Collection, Windsor Castle.

LORENZETTI, PIETRO, SCHOOL OF: Sienese. P.94-95: *Last Supper,* fresco, Lower Church of San Francesco, Assisi.

LUINI, BERNARDINO (?): c.1480-1532, Milanese. P.142: *Mona Lisa* copy, oil on panel, $31\frac{1}{10}$ x 20, Camera dei Deputati, Rome.

MASTER OF THE PALA SFORZESCA: P.62: Portrait of Lodovico Sforza, detail from the *Sforza Altarpiece,* oil and tempera on panel, $90\frac{1}{2}$ x 65, Brera, Milan. Portrait of Beatrice d'Este, detail from the *Sforza Altarpiece.*

Mona Lisa version ("The Nun"). P.142, oil, $29\frac{1}{2}$ x $26\frac{1}{4}$, Vernon Collection, U.S.

Mona Lisa copy. P.142, oil on canvas, $31\frac{1}{4}$ x 25, The Walters Art Gallery, Baltimore.

Mona Lisa copy. P.143, oil, $29\frac{9}{10}$ x $22\frac{2}{5}$, Prado, Madrid.

Mona Lisa, nude version ("La Belle Gabrielle"). P.143, oil on canvas, 30 x 25, Collection of the Earl of Spencer, Althorp, Northampton, England.

Mona Lisa, nude version ("La Flora"). P.143, oil on canvas, $30\frac{7}{10}$ x $23\frac{3}{5}$, Accademia Carrara, Bergamo.

NOLDE, EMIL: 1867-1956, German. P.98-99: *Last Supper,* oil on canvas, $34\frac{5}{8}$ x $42\frac{1}{2}$, Statensmuseum for Kunst, Copenhagen.

PERUGINO, PIETRO: 1445-1523, Central Italian. P.41: *St. Sebastian,* oil on canvas, 67 x 46, Musée du Louvre, Paris.

POLLAIUOLO, ANTONIO DEL: c.1431-1498, Florentine. P.42: *Rape of Deianira,* oil on panel, $23\frac{1}{2}$ x $31\frac{1}{2}$, Yale University Art Gallery, Jarves Collection, New Haven, Conn.

POUSSIN, NICOLAS: c.1594-1665, French. P.97: *Eucharist,* oil on canvas, 46 x 70, The National Gallery of Scotland, lent by the Duke of Sutherland, Edinburgh.

RAPHAEL: 1483-1520, Umbrian. P.127: *Leda and the Swan* (detail), after Leonardo, pen and ink, $12\frac{1}{2}$ x $7\frac{7}{12}$ (whole sheet), Royal Collection, Windsor Castle.

RUSTICI, GIAN FRANCESCO: 1474-1554, Florentine. P.147: *St. John,* bronze, a little over life-size, Baptistery, Florence.

RUBENS, PETER PAUL: 1577-1640, Flemish. P.155: *Fight for the Standard* (after Leonardo), black chalk, pen, gray and white gouache, $17\frac{4}{5}$ x 25, Cabinet des Dessins, Musée du Louvre, Paris.

SPENCER, STANLEY: 1891-1959, British. P.98: *Last Supper,* oil, 36 x 48, Holy Trinity Church, Cookham, England.

Altar frontal of Suriguerola, detail: *Last Supper.* P.94, tempera, $16\frac{1}{2}$ x $42\frac{1}{2}$, Museum of Catalan Art, Barcelona.

TINTORETTO: 1518-1594, Venetian. P.96: *Last Supper,* oil, 11'11" x 18'7", San Giorgio Maggiore, Venice.

VERROCCHIO, ANDREA DEL: 1435-1488, Florentine. P.37: *David,* bronze, height $49\frac{1}{2}$, Museo Nazionale del Bargello, Florence. P.39: *The Colleoni Monument,* bronze, height 13', Campo SS. Giovanni e Paolo, Venice. P.40: *Lady with Primroses,* marble, height 24, Museo Nazionale del Bargello, Florence. P.41: *Boy with Dolphin,* bronze, height without base, 27, Palazzo Vecchio, Florence. P.44: *Baptism of Christ,* panel, $69\frac{7}{8}$ x $59\frac{5}{8}$, Uffizi Gallery, Florence.

Bibliography *Paperback.

CULTURAL AND HISTORICAL BACKGROUND

*Burckhardt, Jacob, *The Civilization of the Renaissance in Italy: An Essay* (2 vols.). Harper Torchbooks, 1960. A pioneering historical characterization of the period.

Chastel, André, *The Age of Humanism: Europe, 1480-1530.* Thames & Hudson, 1963.

Ferguson, Wallace K., *Europe in Transition: 1300-1520.* Allen & Unwin, 1963.

Lucas-Dubreton, Jean, *Daily Life in Florence in the Time of the Medici.* Allen & Unwin, 1960. A highly readable portrait of Florence in the 15th century.

Morley, Lacy Collison, *The Story of the Sforzas.* George Routledge, 1933. One of the few accounts in English of the Sforzas.

Potter, G. R., ed., *The Renaissance: 1493-1520* (*The New Cambridge Modern History,* Vol. I). Cambridge University Press, 1957. A standard historical survey.

*Schevill, Ferdinand, *Medieval and Renaissance Florence* (2 vols.). Harper Torchbooks, 1963. A thorough and readable history, which makes liberal use of contemporary chroniclers so that the flavour of Florence comes through.

Trevelyan, Janet Penrose. *A Short History of the Italian People.* Allen & Unwin, 1956. An informative, interesting and accurate history.

ART HISTORICAL BACKGROUND

*Blunt, Anthony, *Artistic Theory in Italy, 1450-1600.* Oxford University Press, 1962. Texts of Renaissance theories of art, quoted and analysed.

Cenuini, Cennino d'Andrea, *The Craftsman's Handbook.* Translated by Daniel V. Thompson, Jr. Yale University Press: Oxford University Press, 1932-3 (paperback Dover/Constable 1960). Translation of a 15th-century textbook dealing with the techniques and practicalities of the art of painting.

DeWald, Ernest T., *Italian Painting, 1200-1600.* Holt, Rinehart & Winston, New York, 1961.

Freedberg, Sydney, J., *Painting of the High Renaissance in Rome and Florence* (2 vols.). Harvard University Press, 1961. Introduction on Leonardo and the genesis of High Renaissance classic style, and an essay on Leonardo and Michelangelo between 1500 and 1508.

Gould, Cecil, *An Introduction to Italian Renaissance Painting.* Phaidon Press. 1957.

*Hauser, Arnold, *The Social History of Art* (Vol. II). Translated by Stanley Goodman. Routledge, 1962. Comprehensive survey of both art and social history in the 15th, 16th and 17th centuries.

Kennedy, Ruth Wedgwood, *Alesso Baldovinetti, a Critical and Historical Study.* Yale University Press, 1938. An account of Baldovinetti's work, also much material on techniques, other contemporary artists and Renaissance Florentine workshops.

Klein, R. and H. Zermer, *Italian Art 1500-1600: Sources and Documents in the History of Art.* Edited by H. W. Janson. Prentice-Hall, Englewood Cliffs, N.J., 1966.

Murray, Peter, *The Architecture of the Italian Renaissance.* Batsford, 1963.

Pope-Hennessy, John, *Italian Renaissance Sculpture.* Phaidon Press, 1958, new edition, Nov., 1970.

*Vasari, Giorgio, *Lives of the Painters, Sculptors and Architects* (4 vols.). Translated by A. B. Hinds. J. M. Dent (Everyman's Library), 1963. (Also paperback, translated by George Bull. Penguin Books, 1965.)

Wölfflin, Heinrich, *Classic Art: an Introduction to the Italian Renaissance.* Phaidon Press. 1953. By the "father of art history". Translated from the German.

SURVEYS OF RENAISSANCE DRAWINGS

Berenson, Bernard, *The Drawings of the Florentine Painters* (3 vols.). University of Chicago Press, 1938. Amplified edition, richly illustrated; a fundamental work.

LEONARDO, LIFE AND WORK

Brinton, Selwyn. *Leonardo at Milan* (Part VII of *The Renaissance in Italian Art*), G. Bell, 1910. Somewhat old-fashioned, but the only account in English.

*Clark, Sir Kenneth, *Leonardo da Vinci: An account of his development as an artist.* Penguin Books, 1958. The best art historical biography; illustrated.

A Catalogue of the Drawings of Leonardo da Vinci in the Collection of His Majesty the King at Windsor Castle (2 vols.). Cambridge University Press, 1935. One volume of scholarly catalogue, one volume of illustrations for identification purposes.

Eissler, Kurt R., *Leonardo da Vinci; Psychoanalytic Notes on the Enigma.* Hogarth Press: Institute of Psycho-Analysis, 1962. An up-to-date study of the issues raised by Freud.

Goldscheider, Ludwig, *Leonardo da Vinci.* Phaidon Press. 1969. Documents, notes and comments on good, large illustrations of paintings and drawings.

Leonardo da Vinci: Landscapes and Plants. Phaidon Press, 1952.

Heydenreich, Ludwig H., *Leonardo da Vinci.* Allen & Unwin: Macmillan Company, New York, 1955. (Translated from the German.) A total view of Leonardo as artist and scientist.

Leonardo da Vinci Loan Exhibition, Los Angeles County Museum, June 3 to July 17, 1949, Los Angeles, California. An illustrated catalogue.

MacCurdy, Edward, *The Mind of Leonardo da Vinci.* Jonathan Cape, 1952. The most complete single biography of Leonardo.

*Popham, A. E., ed., *The Drawings of Leonardo da Vinci.* Jonathan Cape, 1946. Catalogue and analysis of Leonardo's drawing style.

EVALUATIONS OF LEONARDO

Berenson, Bernard, *The Study and Criticism of Italian Art.* G. Bell, 1930. This includes the essay "Leonardo da Vinci, an Attempt at Re-evaluation".

*Freud, Sigmund, *Leonardo da Vinci and a Memory of his Childhood* (Edited by J. Strachey). Penguin Books, 1963. English translation of Freud's 1910 study in psychosexuality. Although Freud used a faulty translation of Leonardo's notes, knew his works from line-drawn reproductions, and had no sound historical data to rely on, his essay none the less revolutionized the 20th-century concept of the master.

★Pater, Walter, *The Renaissance*. Collins (Fontana Books), 1961. The famous text originally written and printed in *Fortnightly Review*, 1869.

LEONARDO'S MANUSCRIPTS

MacCurdy, Edward, *The Notebooks of Leonardo da Vinci* (2 vols.). Jonathan Cape, 1956. Not as complete as the Richter compilation, but it has a detailed index.

Pedretti, Carlo, ed., *Leonardo da Vinci: Fragments at Windsor Castle from the Codex Atlanticus*. Phaidon Press, 1957.

Richter, Irma A., introduction and English translation, *Paragone, a Comparison of the Arts, by Leonardo da Vinci*. Oxford University Press, 1949.

Richter, Jean Paul, ed., *The Literary Works of Leonardo da Vinci* (2 vols.). Second edition enlarged and revised with the help of Irma A. Richter. Oxford University Press, 1939. All of Leonardo's writings in Italian and English translation.

★Taylor, Pamela, ed., *The Notebooks of Leonardo da Vinci*. New English Library (Mentor) 1961. Selections from the *Treatise on Painting*, with an illuminating introduction.

LEONARDO AS A SCIENTIST

Cooper, Margaret, *The Inventions of Leonardo da Vinci*. The Macmillan Company, New York, 1965. A popular account of Leonardo's inventions.

Hart, Ivor B., *The World of Leonardo da Vinci, Man of Science, Engineer and Dreamer of Flight*. Macdonald, 1961. This is the only book that deals exclusively with Leonardo's science.

O'Malley, Charles D. and J. B. de C. M. Saunders, *Leonardo da Vinci on the Human Body*. Henry Schuman, New York, 1952. Leonardo's anatomical drawings accompanied by his own notes and the authors' explanatory text.

Picture Credits

Acknowledgments

The editors of this book wish to thank the following: Gianalberto dell'Acqua, Soprintendente alle Gallerie delle Provincie Lombarde, Milan; Piero Aranguren, Palazzo Vecchio, Florence; Luisa Becherucci, Soprintendenza alle Gallerie, Florence; Maria Bersano-Begey, Soprintendente, Bibliografica del Piemonte, Turin; Carlo Bertelli, Director, Gabinetto Fotografico Nazionale, Rome; Luciano Berti, Soprintendenza alle Gallerie, Florence; Lidia Bianchi, Director, Gabinetto Nazionale delle Stampe, Rome; Department of Prints and Drawings, British Museum, London; Giulia Bologna, Biblioteca Trivulziana, Milan; Anna Maria Brizio, Raccolta Vinciana, Milan; Budapest Museum of Fine Arts; Luigi Crema, Soprintendente ai Monumenti della Lombardia, Milan; Rodolfo Francioni, Opera del Duomo, Florence; Curator and staff of the Library of the Institut de France, Paris; Interfoto, Budapest; Professor Dr. Walter Koschatzky, Graphische Sammlung, Albertina, Vienna; Kupferstichkabinet, Kunsthalle, Hamburg; Roma Mezzetti, Gabinetto Nazionale delle Stampe, Rome; Bruno Molajoli, Director of Fine Arts and Antiquities for Italy, Ministero di Pubblica Istruzione, Rome; Bianca Musso, Soprintendenza Bibliografica del Piemonte, Turin; Angelo Paredi, Biblioteca Ambrosiana, Milan; Mauro Pellicioli, Milan; Ugo Procacci, Soprintendente ai Monumenti, Florence; The Royal Library, Windsor Castle; Franco Russoli, Director, Pinacoteca Brera, Milan; Silio Sensi, Soprintendenza alle Gallerie, Florence; Maria Todorow, Soprintendenza alle Gallerie, Florence; Franceso Valcanover, Galleria dell'Accademia, Venice; Kabinetsdirektor Dr. Gustav Wilhelm, Vaduz, Liechtenstein.

Index

Numerals in italics indicate a picture of the subject mentioned. Unless otherwise identified, all listed art works are by Leonardo.

Index continued

Finito di stampare nel mese di febbraio 1971 presso le Officine Grafiche Arnoldo Mondadori - Verona - Printed in Italy

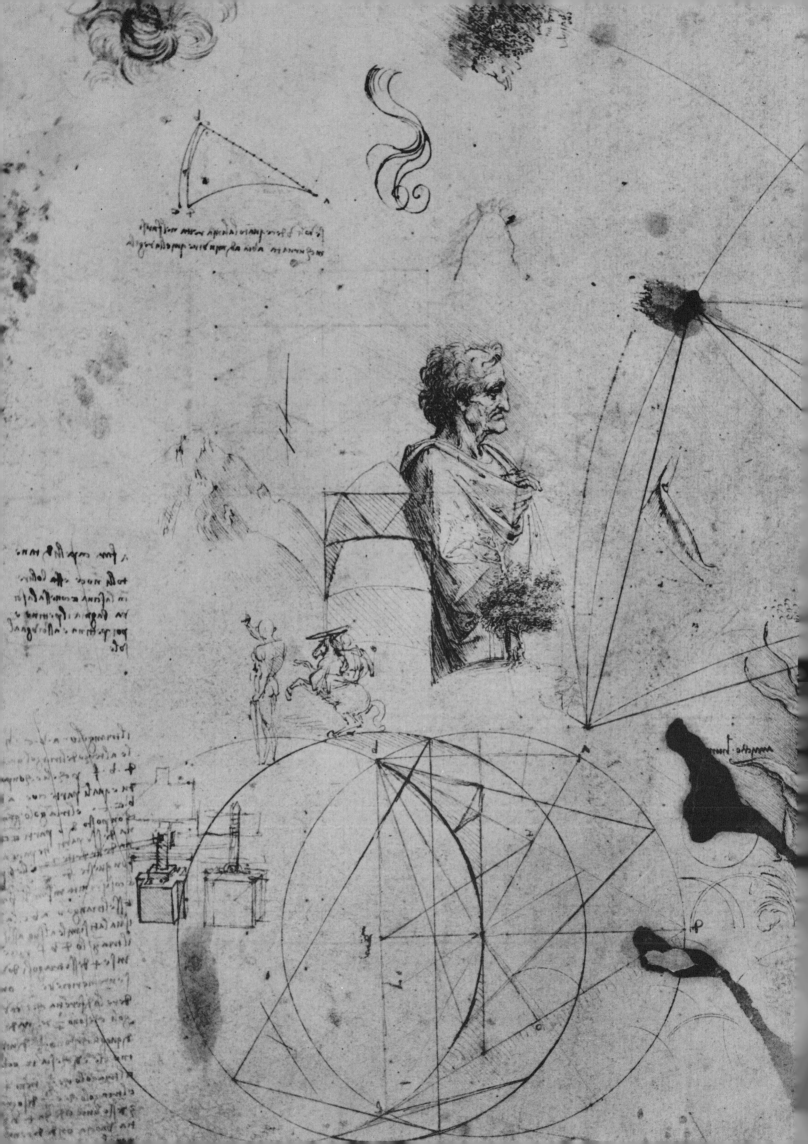